Teaching

INFANTS, TODDLERS, AND TWOS WITH

Special Needs

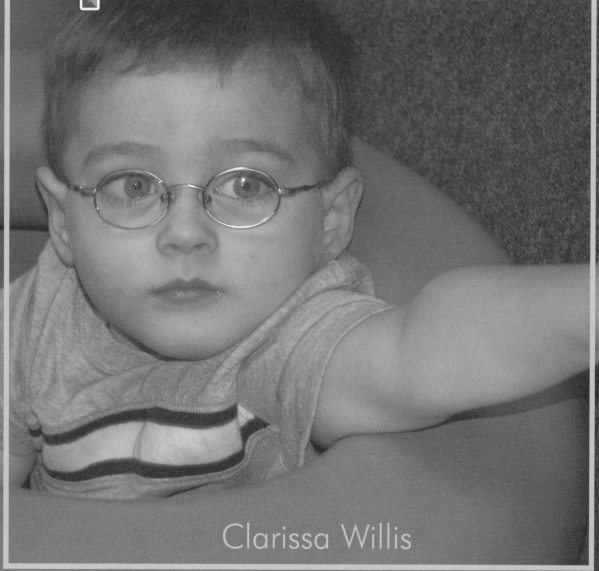

Clarissa Willis

Gryphon House, Inc.
Beltsvieille, MD, USA

Printed in the United States of America.

Published by Gryphon House, Inc.
PO Box 207, Beltsville, MD 20704
301.595.9500; 301.595.0051 (fax); 800.638.0928 (toll-free)

Visit us on the web at www.gryphonhouse.com

Library of Congress Cataloging-in-Publication Data

Willis, Clarissa.
  Teaching infants, toddlers, and twos with special needs / Clarissa Willis
; photographs by Michael O. Talley.
      p. cm.
   ISBN 978-0-87659-069-0
   1. Early childhood special education—United States. 2. Infants with disabilities—Education—United States. I. Title.
   LC4802.W55 2009
   371.9'0472—dc22
                               2009000191

Bulk purchase
Gryphon House books are available for special premiums and sales promotions as well as for fund-raising use. Special editions or book excerpts also can be created to specification. For details, contact the Director of Marketing at Gryphon House.

Disclaimer
Gryphon House, Inc. and the author cannot be held responsible for damage, mishap, or injury incurred during the use of or because of activities in this book. Appropriate and reasonable caution and adult supervision of children involved in activities and corresponding to the age and capability of each child involved, is recommended at all times. Do not leave children unattended at any time. Observe safety and caution at all times.

Every effort has been made to locate copyright and permission information.

Teaching Infants, Toddlers, and Twos with Special Needs

Dedication

This book is dedicated to my nieces and nephews, Eric, Evan, Daisy, and Marly Willis; and Lindsey and Dusty West, and to their grandparents Gene and Zella Willis.

Acknowledgments

Thank you to:
Sheila P. Smith, Ed.D., for your critiquing and editing skills;
Michael L. Willis for your editorial and grammatical skills;
Michael O. Talley for your wonderful pictures;
Donna E. Nelson for your contributions to the chapter on families; and
Miss Beverly and all the children and families at the Child Study Center at East Tennessee State University.

Additional Books by Clarissa Willis

Inclusive Literacy Lessons, with Pam Schiller
Teaching Young Children with Autism Spectrum Disorder

Table of Contents

Teaching Infants, Toddlers, and Twos with Special Needs

Introduction

Teaching Infants, Toddlers, and Twos with Special Needs is designed for all teachers and directors who work with infants, toddlers, and two-year-olds, including special educators and educators working with typically developing children. The content is specifically designed for and directed toward the needs of children with developmental delays, as well as for children who are at-risk for developing special needs. Philosophically, this book supports the understanding that all children can learn, regardless of the challenges they face. Placing children with special needs in environments with their typically developing peers has become more commonplace as continuing research confirms that children benefit and learn from each other and from their teachers. Each chapter in *Teaching Infants, Toddlers, and Twos with Special Needs* includes experiences and activities that are common in settings where infants, toddlers, and two-year-olds learn. Strategies are easy to use and apply to all children. Every attempt has been made to explain the jargon that professionals often use when discussing children with challenges, and to provide examples of how to manage the physical environment and enhance the overall development of young children with special needs.

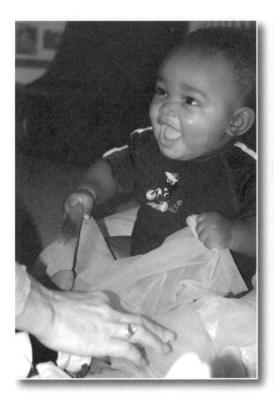

What Do I Do First? Understanding Infants, Toddlers, and Twos with Special Needs

Plan activities that encourage positive interaction with peers.

How Are Infants, Toddlers, and Twos with Special Needs Different from "Typical" Children?

It is important to remember that all children learn at their own pace, and that they all have strengths and weaknesses. Children with special needs are, in many ways, more like their typically developing peers than many people realize. The term **typical**

Note

The first time a term is used in this chapter it appears in bold. All terms in bold are defined at the end of this chapter, beginning on page 20.

development implies that a child falls within a range of development similar to that of other children the same age. Even typically developing infants sometimes lag behind their peers. Therefore, it is important to understand and remember that this normal range is quite broad, and that children will fall somewhere within it. Development depends on many factors, some of which are inherited or genetic in nature, while others are environmental. There are also some conditions, diagnosed at birth, which can indicate that the child will have a **developmental delay**. For example, children with Down syndrome usually have physical characteristics that enable a physician to diagnose them immediately. Certain vision or hearing disorders are often evident at or shortly after birth.

Some conditions, such as **autism spectrum disorder** or **cognitive delays**, are often not diagnosed until after the child develops, often as late as age three or four. In some cases, it is difficult to tell if the delay is just a developmental lag or an ongoing condition. Therefore, the term developmental delay may be used. In other cases, a physician is hesitant to label an infant with a specific diagnosis because she believes the delay may be developmental, and that, under certain circumstances, the child may eventually "catch up" with his peers. With early intervention, such delays may be eliminated. Another factor, which might preclude an immediate diagnosis, may be that the physician suspects the child has a special need, but believes it is too soon to make such a diagnosis. She will instead use the term developmental delay, while continuing to observe the progress of the child. One thing is certain—whether the child has been diagnosed as having a developmental delay or is just considered at-risk for a delay—without a nurturing environment, and without caregivers who are well informed, that child will not reach his full developmental potential.

What Is the Difference Between a Developmental Delay and an At-Risk Infant?

When the term developmental delay is used, it refers to a significant difference between the level at which an infant, toddler, or two-year-old currently functions, and the expected range of development that is based on his chronological age. A developmental delay usually occurs in one or more of the following developmental domains:

- Cognitive
- Motor
- Sensory (including vision and hearing)
- Communication
- Social-emotional
- Adaptive (self-help)

On the other hand, a child may be deemed at-risk, which indicates there is evidence that his environment or some other factor places him in a category where he is likely to develop a temporary or permanent special need. For example, a child who is born to parents who are deaf will be considered at-risk for developing a speech and language delay, given that he may not have the same language learning opportunities available to him as a child who is born to parents who are not deaf. Children living in extreme poverty are also considered at-risk. Research has shown that they may not have access to the same level of health care, nutrition, and learning opportunities as other children. A child who either has a diagnosed condition or is suspected of having an undiagnosed special need is usually referred for **early intervention services**.

What Are Early Intervention Services?

Whether a child has been diagnosed with a developmental delay or a specific special need (Down syndrome, cerebral palsy, and so on), there are laws that determine what services he is entitled to receive. The Individuals with Disabilities Education Act (IDEA) (Public Law 101-476) outlines very specific guidelines that local school districts are required by law to follow when providing for the needs of children with disabilities. The Program for Infants and Toddlers with Disabilities (Part C of IDEA) is a federal grant program that assists states in operating a comprehensive statewide program of early intervention services for infants and toddlers with disabilities serving ages birth through 2 years, and their families. In order for a state to participate in the program it must assure that early intervention will be available to every eligible child and its family. Part C of the IDEA specifies eligibility requirements and sets the criteria for services for children birth to 36 months.

Each state decides if it will serve children who have been diagnosed with developmental delays only, or if it will also serve children with at-risk conditions. In addition, a **lead agency** for Part C is designated by each state. For example, in some states, the lead agency may be the Health Department, while in other states it may be the state's Department of Education or some other government agency. Any child from birth to 36 months can be referred to the lead agency for an eligibility determination. Referrals to the lead agency can come from community members, family members, teachers, care providers, or medical personnel. Once a child has been referred to the lead agency, that agency has, by law, 45 days to complete an eligibility ruling. Every state must provide a toll-free phone number for its Part C lead agency.

After a referral, the child is assigned a **service coordinator**, who has the responsibility of working with the family, medical personnel, and other members of a **multi-disciplinary team**, to coordinate services for which the child is deemed eligible. Each state is responsible for developing its own eligibility standards; eligibility testing is done by a qualified professional, such as a medical doctor, **early interventionist, speech-language pathologist**, or **developmental pediatrician**—usually, at no cost to the child's family. Eligibility is determined with the input of all team members, with the child's parents also included in this multi-disciplinary team. Most states consider a child eligible if he has a diagnosed disability or if he is delayed in one or more of the following domains: cognitive, physical, sensory, communicative, social-emotional, or adaptive.

Many states provide early intervention services for young children who have an established **at-risk condition**, as well as those with developmental delays. An at-risk condition describes an infant, toddler, or two-year-old who has a condition placing him at higher risk for a developmental disability. At-risk conditions may include such factors as low birth-weight and premature birth, and may include infants with respiratory distress or seizure activity during the first weeks of life.

If a child is considered eligible for early intervention (Part C of the IDEA services), the service coordinator works with the family and other professionals to develop an **Individualized Family Service Plan (IFSP)**, a plan written by a team including the child's family. The IFSP outlines the types of services a child will receive (early intervention, speech therapy, occupational therapy, etc.). This plan is reviewed and updated every six months prior to the child's third birthday or until the child is no longer eligible for special education services. When the child turns three he is transitioned into Part B and assuming he is still eligible for special education a new plan called an **Individualized Education Plan (IEP)** is then developed. For all children with special needs, services are provided in the child's **natural environment** or where the child might have spent his time if he did not have a disability. In most cases for children younger than 36 months, the natural environment is at home. However, if both parents work, the natural environment may be a preschool or a private home care provider.

By law, the IFSP must contain the following information:

Holding a toy with both hands is an important concept.

- A statement of the child's present level of functioning, as determined by an appropriate assessment of the developmental domains;
- A family statement outlining the priorities, concerns, challenges, and outcomes that are deemed important for the child's development;
- An outcome statement, with timelines, that details what the plan is for the child. For example, to be able to speak 20 words by a certain date, or to be able to bring his hands to midline, and so on;
- A specific list of the early intervention services needed by the child and his family, which might include support in the areas of speech therapy, nutritional counseling, or physical therapy;
- A statement of the intensity, duration, and method in which early intervention services are to be provided to the child and his family;
- Information about the natural environment where services will be provided, and a statement of justification, if those services will not be provided in the natural environment;
- The name of the **service coordinator**, usually employed by the lead agency, who is in charge of implementing and monitoring the IFSP and its components;
- An outline of the ongoing review, evaluation, and any needed plan revisions; and

- A statement about what is planned for the child when he turns three—usually referred to as a **transition statement**.

Before the child's third birthday, a transition conference is held to determine if the child is eligible to continue receiving services through the public school. Under IDEA, public schools are mandated to provide services for children with disabilities between the ages of 3 and 21. Part B of IDEA provides services for children ages 3–5; these services are the responsibility of the child's local school district.

What Types of Developmental Delays Might I See in My Classroom?

For the purposes of this book, the term developmental delay will be used to describe all types of disabilities that may be encountered in a setting serving infants, toddlers, and two-year-olds. However, there are some types of developmental delays that are seen more common. These include (but are not limited to) infants with:

- Cognitive delays, as observed in children with Down syndrome or mental retardation;
- Physical delays, as with infants, toddlers, or two-year-olds who have cerebral palsy or motor issues;
- Communication delays, such as those observed with infants, toddlers, or two-year-olds who do not develop speech skills or do not communicate;
- Sensory impairments, such as with infants, toddlers, or two-year-olds who experience vision or hearing loss. While rare, this also refers to children who are **dual sensory impaired**, meaning the child is both hearing and vision impaired; and
- Social-emotional delays, as seen in children with autism spectrum disorder.

What Types of Tests or Assessments Will I Be Expected to Give?

Generally, assessments administered for eligibility purposes are given by professionals, such as early interventionists or developmental specialists. However, you may be asked to administer a test designed to determine how the child is functioning developmentally. These tests are usually given as checklists that determine how the child is functioning in specific domains. Popular developmental assessments include

Toddlers enjoy activities that involve jumping and throwing.

the Denver Developmental Screening Test, the Carolina Infant-Toddler Curriculum Test, and the Developmental Assessment of Young Children (DAYC). In addition, you may be asked by the child's early interventionist or service coordinator to complete a checklist about the child's eating and/or sleeping habits or about his self-help skills. The National Early Childhood Technical Assistance Center has information about assessments that you might use to help plan for a child with developmental delays. See www.nectac.org/topics/earlyid/screeneval.asp for more information.

What If a Child Has Not Been Diagnosed with a Special Need?

Even if a child has not been diagnosed with a disability, you and the child can still benefit from the strategies presented in this book. Some specific disabilities (such as autism spectrum disorder) may not be diagnosed before the child is three. Please keep in mind that even if a child has some of the characteristics of a specific disability, the diagnosis must come from a medical professional. You may suggest that a parent call their local Part C service provider and request an evaluation, or with the parent's permission, you may contact that agency on behalf of the family. However, whether or not a child is ultimately evaluated is a family decision.

Where Do I Begin?

After you have learned that a child with special needs will be in your classroom, the first step is to develop an attitude of full inclusion. You should develop both a philosophy and an attitude that all children can learn, and that children learn best in settings with their typically developing peers. Think about the following statements, as you prepare to become involved in the life of an infant, toddler, or two-year-old with a developmental delay:

1. An infant with a developmental delay is not "broken." In other words, that child does not need to be "repaired" or "fixed" before he can benefit from being in a setting with his peers. It is important to recognize that every child is unique, regardless of the challenges he faces.
2. Young children grow up in a world where everyone is not the same. Even infants, toddlers, and two-year-olds can learn to be tolerant and accepting of others, especially those with developmental delays.
3. For your program to be successful, it must reflect a team approach to planning for an infant, toddler, or two-year-old with developmental delays. You should welcome and encourage the input and ongoing involvement of all participants, especially the child's family.
4. Inclusive programs model the belief that all children are entitled to experience developmentally appropriate materials and exemplary classroom practices that value the child's strengths and work to improve the child's weaknesses.
5. It is important to understand that no single method, process, or product works for every child. This includes an understanding that working with infants,

toddlers, and two-year-olds with developmental delays is about following a process, and not about "buying" a specific product.

6. Quality programs for infants, toddlers, and two-year-olds with special needs will allow you to recognize when something works, and to be able to change and adapt when something does not work. It is okay to recognize that active involvement with the child sometimes involves "trial and error." When an approach or a method is not successful, change it!

General Guidelines for Working with Infants, Toddlers, and Twos with Developmental Delays

- *Model a belief that every child in your classroom is important.*
  - o Children learn by imitating what others do and say. It is important for the other children in your class to see that you view all children, especially children with disabilities, as valuable class members who are important, not only to you, but that all class members are also important to each other.
  - o Use **people-first language** when talking about a child. Refer to the child first and the disability last. For example, Brianna is a child with Down syndrome—she is not the "Down syndrome child." Derrick is a child with a visual challenge—he is not a "blind child."
  - o During discussions, never talk about the child with disabilities as though he does not exist or is not present. The child should be included in conversations in the same way that any child would be. Parents of children with disabilities appreciate support from people who value their child and who treat him respectfully in a positive, reinforcing manner.
- *Help typically developing infants, toddlers, and twos accept their peers with developmental delays.*
  - o Look for ways to help the infant, toddler, or two-year-old with delays participate in everyday activities and routines. If the child cannot fully participate at the same level as his peers, look for ways to adapt an activity in a way that allows him to **partially participate**.
  - o In your classroom, read stories that feature people with disabilities as members of the community. To help facilitate this, you could display pictures around the classroom that depict people with disabilities who are participating with and contributing to their community.
  - o Remember that all children can learn. Some children just take more time and practice.

Toddlers with visual challenges enjoy exploring real objects.

Terms Used in This Chapter

at-risk condition—An infant who has a condition that places him at risk (or increases the likelihood) for the development of a disability.

autism spectrum disorder—Refers to the whole range of symptoms that are characteristic of autism. These characteristics will differ and can range from very mild to quite severe.

cognitive delay—Significantly sub-average intellectual abilities coupled with deficits in functional or self-help skills.

developmental delay—A young child who is currently functioning below the expected range of development for his or her chronological age.

developmental pediatrician—A medical doctor who diagnoses and treats children with conditions that are associated with their development

dual sensory impaired—Term used to describe an individual who has two or more senses (usually vision and hearing) which are impaired.

early intervention services—Services provided by a professional, such as an early interventionist, speech-language pathologist, or occupational therapist, to a child between the ages of birth and 36 months.

early interventionist—Term used to describe a person who works with children usually age birth to three who need help reaching developmental milestones. These services are often but not always delivered in the child's home environment.

Individualized Education Plan (IEP)—A plan written for every child age 3–21 who is receiving special education services through the public education system. This plan details the services that child will receive, the amount of time the child will receive those services (once a week, daily etc) and the least restrictive environment in which those services will be provided. This plan must be reviewed on an annual basis.

Individualized Family Service Plan (IFSP)—A written plan by a team including the child's family which outlines the services that a child will receive while in Part C (Birth through age 2). This plan is reviewed every six months and helps guide the family as the child transitions between programs.

Individuals with Disabilities Education Act (IDEA) (Public Law 101-476)—A Federal law that outlines very specific guidelines that local school districts are required to follow when providing for the needs of children with disabilities.

lead agency—The agency designated by a state to handle referrals and to determine eligibility for a child who is diagnosed with a developmental delay.

multi-disciplinary team—A team (including the child's family) that determines eligibility for services and plans and implements support services for a child with a developmental delay. Members of this team may include (but are not limited to) a medical doctor, an early interventionist, a speech-language pathologist, and a developmental pediatrician.

natural environment—The place where the child might spend her time if she did not have a disability.

partially participate—When a child cannot fully complete an activity, the modification of the activity will allow the child to participate partially and to the best of his ability.

people-first language—Language used when referring to a child, which ensures that a child with a developmental delay is referred to as being a child (person) first, and that having the disability is considered to be secondary. For example, a child with developmental delays rather than a "delayed child."

service coordinator—An employee of the lead agency who works with the family, appropriate medical personnel, and other members of a multi-disciplinary team, to determine eligibility and to coordinate services for children birth to 36 months who are eligible for Part C services under IDEA.

speech-language pathologist—A specialist trained to work with children with speech and/or language delays.

transition statement—A statement that outlines how a child will be transitioned or moved from one setting to another.

typical development—A child whose development is within the range considered by experts to be within the same range as that of other children who are the same age.

Resources Used in This Chapter

Blasco, P. (2001). *Early intervention services of infants, toddlers and their families.* Needham Heights, MA: Allyn & Bacon.

Segal, M. (1988). *In time with love: Caring for the special needs baby.* New York: New Market Press.

Willis, C. (2006). *Teaching young children with autism spectrum disorder.* Beltsville, MD: Gryphon House.

For More Information

Balaban, N. (2006). Easing the separation process for infants, toddlers, and families. *Young Children*, 61(1), 14–20.

Blind Children's Center, Los Angeles, CA. (2007). *Blind children's center annual report*, 2006–2007 Blind Children's Center. 4120 Marathon Street, Los Angeles, CA 90029-3584. Tel: 323-664-2153; Fax: 323-665-3828; Website: www.blindchildrenscenter.org/pubs_res.htm www.blindchildrenscenter.org/annual.htm

Danaher, J., Goode, S., & Lazara, A. (2007). *Part C updates: 9th edition.* National Early Childhood Technical Assistance Center (NECTAC). Campus Box 8040, UNC-CH, Chapel Hill, NC 27599-8040. Tel: 919-962-2001; Fax: 919-966-7463; email: nectac@unc.edu; Website: www.nectac.org/pubs/pubs.asp

Loewenstein, D. (2007). Increasing our acceptance as parents of children with special needs. *Exceptional Parent*, 37(12), 28–29.

Neuharth-Pritchett, S. (2007). Research into practice: Interventions for infants, toddlers, and preschoolers. *Journal of Research in Childhood Education*, 22(1), 97. Retrieved from www.acei.org.

Year One—
The Journey Begins

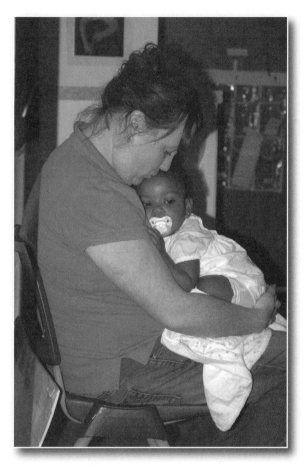

*Bonding with a caring adult is a critical
early skill for an infant.*

When there is a degree of certainty, families may learn early on that their child has a syndrome or chronic medical condition. In other cases, what might at first appear to indicate something atypical will later simply establish itself as having been part of the child's normal birth process. For example, first-time parents are sometimes surprised that their newborn baby does not look or act exactly the way they expected. It may be that the child's physical appearance seems distorted or perhaps swollen. This may be the normal result of going through the dynamics of the birth process, or it may simply be due to the infant's physical immaturity. For example, most babies who are born vaginally will have a physically distorted head. This distortion, or **molding**, occurs when bones in the skull shift and overlap, making the top of the infant's head appear elongated, stretched out, or even pointed. Molding is a temporary condition, which usually subsides

─ Note ─

The first time a term is used in this chapter it appears in bold. All terms in bold are defined at the end of this chapter, beginning on page 32.

within 48 hours of birth. Additionally, after a long and difficult labor, there may be some swelling of the scalp, which is caused by the pressure of the baby's head against the mother's cervix. This swelling is referred to as **caput succedaneum**. This too, will gradually disappear soon after birth.

Parents may also be concerned because a newborn has large bruises on her head. This bruising is referred to as a **cephalhematoma** and results from blood vessels that break during the birth process. However, unlike the other conditions mentioned, these bruises may take several months to heal. It is important that care providers keep an eye on such bruises. If sudden swelling appears or if the bruise does not heal, medical attention may be required.

What Factors Determine If a Child Is High Risk for a Special Need?

There are certain conditions that can result in the infant being classified as high risk. This does not necessarily mean the child will have a developmental delay. It does, however, mean that the infant has a greater likelihood of developing future problems as a result of a high-risk condition. Some common high-risk conditions include:

- *Birth weight*: It is important to distinguish between premature infants and those with **low birth weight (LBW)**, which is used to describe infants who weigh less than five pounds, eight ounces. Consequently, **very low birth weight** is used to describe infants weighing less than three pounds, four ounces, or 1,500 grams.
- *Size at birth*: **Small for gestational age (SGA)** describes an infant who is much smaller than usual for the number of weeks of pregnancy. An example would be a child who, born after 38–40 weeks, is abnormally smaller than 90% of her peers. SGA can occur when the infant has suffered **intrauterine growth retardation (IUGR)**. IUGR occurs when the fetus does not receive the necessary nutrients and oxygen required for proper growth and development of organs and tissues; it can begin at any time during pregnancy. Early-onset IUGR is often due to chromosomal abnormalities, maternal disease, or severe problems with the placenta. Late-onset growth restriction (after 32 weeks) is usually related to other problems such as exposure to chemicals or other poisonous substances.

Both genetic predisposition and the mother's prenatal care, including nutrition during pregnancy, can affect the infant's weight and/or size at birth. The average weight for a full-term (38–40 weeks) infant is approximately seven pounds, three ounces. Newborns diagnosed as high risk may experience one or more of the following medical conditions:

- Respiratory conditions (breathing problems)
- Neurological conditions (brain or nervous system issues)
- Gastrointestinal problems (trouble eating or swallowing)

- Developmental problems (challenges in learning new things or reaching developmental milestones)

It is important to know if a child is classified as high-risk. In order to know when it is necessary to contact medical personnel, it is equally worthwhile to know what is normal for the child, to learn to read the child's signals, and to become keen observers of newborns.

What Do You Mean by "Learn to Read the Newborn's Signals"?

With careful observation, you can learn that newborns are very good at developing a series of signals to let those around them know what they want or need. For example, a newborn might calm herself by sucking her thumb or curling up into a fetal position. It is also important to recognize and respond accordingly to an infant's behavioral patterns. The most commonly observed behavioral states include:

- *Deep sleep*, in which the infant is breathing regularly and is relaxed with her eyes closed. In this state, the infant is unbothered by the world around her, and experiences the rest she requires to keep her mind and body functioning properly;
- *Normal active sleep*, sometimes referred to as **REM (rapid eye movement) sleep**, which occurs when the infant is sleeping calmly and breathing evenly but may move her body while she sleeps;
- *Light sleep*, in which breathing in an irregular manner and where she might startle once or twice for no apparent reason. In this state, the baby may be aware of sounds around her, and often struggles to return to a state of deep sleep;
- A *semi-alert state* occurs when the infant is drowsy. In this state, her eyes may flutter open then shut. This is usually a predecessor to sleep and the infant should not be aroused or startled by loud noises or activity;
- A *quiet-alert state* occurs when the infant begins to adapt to her immediate environment. She is excited by an object or person and may show her interest by breathing rapidly or deeply. During this state, the infant may gaze at an adult's face, follow an object with her eyes and head, or move in an organized manner;
- A *fussy wide-awake state*, in which the infant is wide-eyed and is full of movement. This activity may

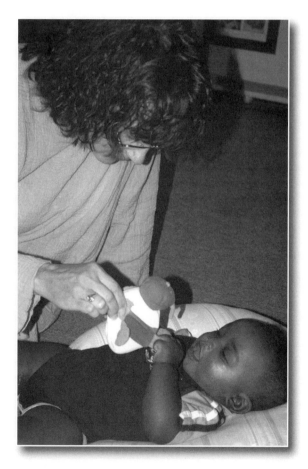

Interacting helps build trust.

appear to be erratic, and is usually a result of the infant's being unable to control her momentary feelings and needs; and

- *A fussy-crying state*, where the infant is breathing irregularly and her movements are jerky and uncontrolled. She may even thrash about and scream loudly. This fussiness is a normal part of the developmental process. When the child reaches this state, it may take a tremendous effort to calm her down and often the result will be less than desired.

It can be very challenging when you are responsible for a high-risk infant. Because the long-term complications for a specific child may be unknown, you may be hesitant to make the effort required to attend to a child labeled as at-risk. However, as with infants who are not high risk, these children will respond to attentive care and stimulating environments. It is, however, essential to build a positive and trusting relationship with the child. This will develop over time as the child's needs and desires become more apparent.

Interactions with Infants

Two of the most well-known infant specialists, Brazelton and Cramer (1990), describe a theoretical model of relationship-building that is applicable to both parents and caregivers. Table 2–1 on the following page shows a summary of their model.

Attachment

Infants enter into a world that is new and, in some ways, very frightening for them. Attachment theory has long suggested that infants will inherently seek adult attachments to help them adapt to their new environment. However, because some children may also have a special need, such as a developmental delay or a chronic health issue, they may be unable to form attachments in the traditional manner. As a result, the child with special needs may enter a new child care setting with various attachment issues. For example, the infant may not have had enough time to develop a secure base with a caregiver, and may, therefore, be fearful of attempting new activities. Secure attachment patterns are usually developed during the child's first year. An infant will become attached to the primary caregiver(s) or to a person on whom they consistently depend for human contact, food, and comfort. If you have no previous experience working with children with special needs, you may not fully understand how to help the child feel attached and secure. Use the following suggestions to help infants develop secure attachments:

- Provide a secure base for the child, as she begins to explore the world around her.
- Allow extra time so that interactions can occur. Because a child with special needs may take extra time while engaging in activities, such as eating and basic toileting, there may be a tendency to avoid taking the necessary additional time to interact and talk with the child.

Table 2-1 *Brazelton and Cramer's (1990) Theoretical Model of Relationship-Building*

Phases of Relationship Building	Characteristics	Suggestions for Interactions
Synchrony	The infant cries for attention and to have her needs met. Synchrony occurs as adults respond to those cries and become more confident that they can meet the infant's needs. It is considered by some to be the first real phase of infant bonding and attachment.	• Be as nurturing as possible. • Treat each cry as a real need. • Observe the baby's movements and soothe her when she is "fussy." This helps the child learn to trust the adults in her world.
Symmetry	Adults learn more about what interests the infant and look for opportunities to interact with her. The child begins to focus and direct her attention more toward the people in her world.	• Use mutual gaze to engage the child's attention. • Find objects that interest her.
Contingency	At this stage, infants begin to use multiple methods, such as smiles or "coos," to interact with adults. Some babies as young as six weeks may develop a movement or look as a signal to play.	• Talk or sing to the child and wait for her response. • Learn gestures, movements, or expressions that make the infant smile and look at you.
Play	As early as three or four months of age, an infant may begin to interact with adults through play. This "play" is usually an interaction initiated by either the child or the adult.	• Imitation and modeling can be challenging if the infant has special needs. • She may not respond in a typical manner. Learn to read the infant's cues and respond to the slightest movement. • Always position the child in such a way that she can see your face.
Autonomy and Flexibility	By five months of age, most infants initiate and stop interactions, either by rolling over, turning away, or protesting loudly. At this stage, the infant will develop more visual, auditory, and motor skills and will use them interchangeably.	• Provide a safe environment for exploration. • Continue to respond to the child's movements and vocalizations. • Learn to watch for cues that she is getting too tired or is bored with an activity.

- Be physically and emotionally available to meet the child's needs. From this basis of security, the child will trust that they are safe, and that their needs will be met warmly, consistently, and reliably. The child's anxiety is reduced and she gains the confidence to explore her world, secure with the knowledge that care and protection will be available in times of need.
- Respond with sensitivity to the child's feelings. This conveys your ability to understand and empathize with what the child may be thinking and feeling.
- Recognize the child as a unique individual whose wishes, feelings, and goals are valid and meaningful. Look for ways to promote the child's capacity to make choices (within clear boundaries), while working to cooperate with the child wherever possible.
- Accept the child and build her self-esteem. Communicate the message that the child is unconditionally accepted and valued for who she is, for her difficulties as well as strengths. This provides a foundation of positive self-esteem so the child believes herself to be worthy of receiving love, help, and support, as well as having the ability to deal confidently with challenges and setbacks when they occur.
- Promote family membership to help children feel that they belong. It is vitally important to communicate to the child her importance as a family member, both socially and as an individual. In other words, always aim toward helping the child establish an appropriate sense of connectedness and belonging in her family at home, as well as in her "family" of the child care environment. In this way, the child, who is likely, at times, to feel some degree of uncertainty or perhaps divided loyalties, can more easily develop a comfortable sense of belonging in both settings.

Understanding attachment theory can increase the confidence of adoptive and foster parents by helping them understand the child and giving them a sense of direction as well. With help from their new families, children who are adopted can change their ways of thinking, feeling, and behaving. Even with something as simple as when a child first asks for a helping hand or accepts praise in her new family setting, one can begin to see the powerful effects that caring relationships can have on a child. With positive parenting strategies, which help children feel more trusting, manage their behavior, and think through their feelings, children from even the most difficult backgrounds can become more secure and resilient. Bailey and Wolery (1992) summarized the rationale for positive caregiver infant/child interactions in this way:

- Early relationships may influence overall development.
- There appears to be a strong relationship between secure attachments and positive social outcomes for the future.
- Special needs may reduce an infant's capacity to engage in rewarding interactions.
- An infant's special needs may pose interactive difficulties and may make adults reluctant to interact with an infant.
- Mutually satisfying interactions may be the basis from which other positive interventions stem.

The following suggestions can help you plan positive interactions with infants with special needs:

- Plan activities that require taking turns or a give-and-take. For example, hold a brightly colored object in the child's line of vision and wiggle it back and forth. When the infant reaches or moves her body toward the object, hand it to her. Encourage her to shake the object and hand it back to you.
- Adjust to the child's cues. If she looks away, assume the game is over.
- Imitate what the child does and encourage her to imitate you.
- Play games, sing songs, and talk to the child.
- Use facial expressions that indicate you are enjoying the activity.
- Recognize that children with special needs may not respond in typical ways. Learn to identify how the child lets you know that she is finished, wants more of an activity, or wants to change an activity.

The Role of Temperament

Traditionally, temperament in infants has been defined as the individual differences that occur in how an infant behaves or expresses her emotions. Temperament can affect how an infant responds to her environment as well as to those around her. One of the first signs of socialization is the social smile. Caregivers and family members often confuse the **social smile** with the reflexive smile. Infants will often smile using the muscles around the mouth, which may be just a reflex (reflexive smile). According to Blasco (2001), the social smile involves the muscles of the mouth and eyes, and occurs as a response to a person or a pleasurable activity. You can help the child by responding to her social smile with a smile and warm greeting; your response reinforces the child's use of the social smile, which is an indication of a positive temperament.

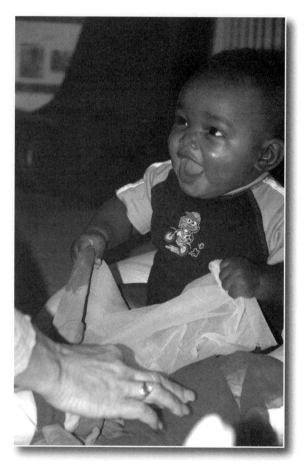

As mentioned, temperament is also reflected in a child's response to or disposition in a given environment. For example, during the first three months of life, a typically developing infant will become less fussy and will experience increasingly longer periods of alertness. However, an infant with special needs may have more difficulty remaining alert and focused. Unfortunately, this may cause you to hesitate to properly engage the child with special needs. It is important to attempt to engage the child, even if for short periods, while recognizing that she may require more time for resting than her typically developing peers.

Infants often communicate nonverbally with a smile.

Exploration and Motivation

As infants grow and develop, they enjoy exploring new toys and activities.

As an infant matures and develops, her interest in objects and people increases. She begins to use her hands and mouth to manipulate objects, and "talks" to an adult with coos and babbling noises. By six months of age, many infants are able to imitate a vowel sound made by an adult and will consistently make some consonant-vowel combinations, such as "ba-ba" or "da-da." A six-month-old will roll over and play games like pat-a-cake or peek-a-boo. Once she can sit up by herself, a whole new world opens up for her to explore. As her mobility increases, her environment continues to grow even larger, and she begins to actively explore everything within reach. It is during the first year of life that cause and effect, one of the earliest and most important cognitive skills, is mastered.

Alternatives for Children with Special Needs

Children with motor difficulties or visual disabilities need assistance in developing alternative methods for exploring their environment. Those with visual impairments who have some residual vision will need to have toys and objects presented directly to them, within their line of vision. In addition, toys and objects should make noise and be brightly colored. For children with motor challenges, it is very important that they have as much room for mobility as possible. Work closely with a physical therapist to insure that the child is positioned in such a way that she has a wide range of motion. For children who are unable to sit up alone, you will need additional instruction on how to support their head and trunk.

Cause and effect, or learning that an action can cause a reaction, is a very important concept. For example, when a child wiggles her hands and feet, the mobile overhead is activated by her movement and begins to move and play a tune. Because it is important to understand cause and effect, children with special needs should participate in activities that allow them to explore and practice cause-and-effect experiences as often as possible. For example:

- Provide a toy or object that lights up or blinks when the infant moves it and stops blinking when the infant stops moving it.
- Place a rattle in the infant's line of vision and shake it. Then, give the rattle to the infant and see if she will imitate your movements to make it rattle. If she doesn't, place your hand gently over her hand and repeat the activity.

- Respond to the infant's babbles by repeating back to her the same sounds that she just made.
- Rock the child gently back and forth in your arms, and then stop. If she moves her body as though she doesn't want you to stop, respond to her by saying, "Oh, you want more rocking!"

General Suggestions for Infants with Developmental Challenges

- *Follow the child's lead.* Try to engage the child by using objects that interest her. Being able to determine the specific interests of a child with multiple disabilities or a sensory loss, such as vision or hearing, may be challenging. Sometimes, you may need to use objects that are very bright, made of exaggerated textures, or those that are very colorful.
- *Look for opportunities throughout daily routines* that encourage children to make choices. For example, present two objects to the child; if she leans or reaches for one, interpret her movement as a choice. Reinforce the choice by giving the child the toy.
- *Use natural consequences.* The infant must learn the natural consequence for an action, such as when she activates a pull toy, the toy moves. In addition, when you smile at her, she receives the additional reinforcement of a positive response from a caring adult, which may be a smile, gesture, hug, or clapping your hands in excitement and approval.
- *Respond consistently.* One of the most critical elements involved in the child's learning to trust her world and the people in it is the consistency to which her early attempts at communication are reinforced. Therefore, it is vital that you respond to her crying, movements, and smiles.
- *Set the child up to succeed.* Design activities that she can complete successfully. For example, when teaching a child to reach across her midline (the middle of her body) to grab a toy, make sure the toy is of interest to her and that she can grasp it easily.
- *Break tasks into manageable steps.* Children find new tasks easier to complete if they are able to approach them in smaller, easy-to-accomplish segments.
- *Provide opportunities for practice.* For example, when you roll a ball to an infant who is sitting on the floor and she makes no attempt to roll it back to you, it may be that she simply needs a demonstration. Ask another adult to sit behind the child, place her hands over the child's hands, and gently roll the ball back to you. Even if the ball just rolls in your general direction, reach for it, smile, and roll the ball back to the child. Encourage the other adult to sit back and see if the child will attempt to roll the ball by herself. If she does not, ask the adult to assist her again. Practice is important; it may take some time for the child to attempt to roll the ball alone.
- *Use daily routines as times to learn.* For example, if you are trying to teach a child to grasp an object and bring it to midline, look for ways to do this while you are feeding her, playing with her, or reading to her.

- *Allow the child time to rest and reflect.* Because some children with special needs will use great amounts of energy when responding, they may require longer periods to rest and "re-energize" themselves. Make sure there is a quiet place for the child to rest.
- *Work collaboratively with the child's family.* Families are the most informative collaborative partners you have. Develop ways to communicate with them about the child's challenges as well as her successes. Encourage families to let you know what is going on at home, and make you aware of simple things, such as changes in sleep patterns or eating habits. This information can have an enormous impact on how you can better understand and care for the child with special needs, as well as how the child responds to your care.

Terms Used in This Chapter

caput succedaneum—A swelling of the scalp, caused by the pressure of the baby's head on the mother's cervix, which disappears gradually after birth.

cephalhematoma—Bruises on the head that occur at birth as the result of blood vessels breaking during the birth process. These bruises may take several months to heal.

intrauterine growth retardation (IUGR)—IUGR occurs when the fetus does not receive the necessary nutrients and oxygen required for proper growth and development of organs and tissues; it can begin at any time during pregnancy.

low birth weight (LBW)—Infants weighing less than five pounds, eight ounces, at birth.

molding—When the bones in the skull shift and overlap during delivery, the top of the infant's head looks elongated, stretched out, or even pointed at birth. Molding is a temporary condition, which usually subsides within 48 hours of birth.

REM (rapid eye movement) sleep—Often referred to as normal deep sleep, REM sleep occurs when the infant breathes in a regular manner and sleeps without much movement.

small for gestational age (SGA)—An infant who is much smaller than usual for the number of weeks of pregnancy.

social smile—A smile which occurs in response to person or a pleasurable activity. Many consider a social smile to be a major developmental milestone for an infant because it is intentional as well as responsive.

very low birth weight—Infants weighing less than three pounds, four ounces or 1,500 grams at birth.

Resources Used in This Chapter

Bailey, D. B., & Wolery, M. (1992). *Teaching infants and preschoolers with disabilities.* Upper Saddle River, NJ: Prentice-Hall.

Blasco, P. M. (2001). *Early intervention services for infants, toddlers, and their families.* Boston: Allyn and Bacon.

Brazelton, T. B., & Cramer, B. G. (1990). *The earliest relationship: Parents, infants, and the drama of early attachment*. Reading, MA: Addison Wesley.

For More Information

Cotton, J. N., Edwards, C. P., Zhao, W., & Gelabert, J. M. (2007). Nurturing care for china's orphaned children. *Young Children*, 62(6), 58–60, 62–63.

Dallaire, D. H., & Weinraub, M. (2007). Infant-mother attachment security and children's anxiety and aggression at first grade. *Journal of Applied Developmental Psychology*, 28(5–6), 477–492.

Leach, P., Barnes, J., Malmberg, L., Sylva, K., & Stein, A. (2008). The quality of different types of child care at 10 and 18 months: A comparison between types and factors related to quality. *Early Child Development and Care*, 178(2), 177–209.

Matthews, D., Lieven, E., & Tomasello, M. (2007). How toddlers and preschoolers learn to uniquely identify referents for others: A training study. *Child Development*, 78(6), 1744–1759.

Naber, F. B. A., Swinkels, S. H. N., Buitelaar, J. K., Dietz, C., van Daalen, E., Bakermans-Kranenburg, M. J., et al. (2007). Joint attention and attachment in toddlers with autism. *Journal of Abnormal Child Psychology*, 35(6), 899–911.

Turati, C., Bulf, H., & Simion, F. (2008). Newborns' face recognition over changes in viewpoint. *Cognition*, 106(3), 1300–1321.

Older Infants, Toddlers, and Twos

Provide real objects when possible.

Older Infants

As children move out of early infancy, they become more confident, exert more energy exploring the world around them, and become increasingly independent. Major changes occur physically, intellectually, and emotionally. Children between the ages of 12 and 18 months may:

- Attempt to solve a new problem using trial and error,
- Follow a simple command,
- Imitate an action after watching it modeled,
- Understand that when an object is removed from view or is hidden under a cloth, the object still exists (object permanence), or
- Combine one or two actions to complete a goal, such as stacking blocks or throwing a ball.

Note

The first time a term is used in this chapter it appears in bold. All terms in bold are defined at the end of this chapter, beginning on page 45.

Children at this stage of development depend heavily on their senses to help them solve problems. Given this, it makes sense that a child with a sensory loss will need extra support in order to learn many of these skills. Children with various types of special needs may exhibit some or all of these behaviors, but usually at a much slower rate than their peers. These are a few adaptations that can help a child with special needs learn the important skills mentioned:

- *Solve a new problem using trial and error.* Try modeling for the child how to solve the problem. For example, if you want a child to put a block into a container, first demonstrate the skill for him. Place your hand over his hand and gently guide it toward the container. Encourage the child to drop the block inside. You may need to repeat the demonstration several times before the child can do the task independently. Remember to praise the child for each attempt even if it is not successful. This technique is called **successive approximation** or **shaping**. When he receives praise for close approximations, it encourages him to keep trying.

- *Follow a simple command.* Often, children with special needs do not understand what you are asking them to do. To help them understand better, use multiple cues, such as pointing, modeling, and pictures. As mentioned, you may have to show the child how to do something several times before he is able to complete the task or solve the problem. One reason children with special needs may need multiple cues is because they often do not **generalize** well. That is, they may have difficulty recognizing that a task is performed the same way in various settings. For example, most children understand that a routine, such as getting ready for small group time, may be performed the same way each day. However, a child with special needs may not be able to comprehend such routines. If you find this with a particular child, you may need to demonstrate for him each day that, when you say, "Time for circle," he should finish what he is doing and join the group. That is why **daily schedule picture cards** can be especially useful for children with special needs.

- *Imitate an action after watching it modeled.* To help children with special needs imitate actions, such as clapping their hands to music or standing up when their name is called, it is important to break the action into simple steps and demonstrate each one for the child. Remember, with practice and patience, all children can learn. Even if a child cannot fully participate in an activity, he can always partially participate, often with the use of specific adaptations. For example, a child who has severe motor delays may not be able to dance to music, but he may be able to wave a scarf while others dance.

- *Explore object permanence.* Because children with special needs often do not generalize well, it is important to set up activities that help them learn about object permanence. One way to do this is to play games, such as "Cup Hide and Seek." Play the game by placing two cups upside down on a table. While the child is watching, take a small object, place it under one cup, and slowly move the cups around. Ask the child to guess which cup the object is under (let the child see clearly which cup the object is under by either lifting up the cup and giving the child a "hint" or by allowing the child to watch you while you place the item under the cup. Use variations on this activity, such as placing a small block under one of two cloths, placing a ball behind one of two books, and so on.

- *Combine one or two actions to complete a goal.* As mentioned, a child with special needs will usually need additional cues and practice to complete his task or accomplish his goal. Use gestures or **picture sequence cards** as a way to show him what you want him to do. Breaking a task into smaller steps and modeling each step for him can also be extremely helpful. Remember to use **shaping** to reinforce each approximation toward the final goal that the child achieves.

Physical Changes Between 12 and 36 Months

In terms of motor development (see Chapter 10 for a full description), it is during this time that much new and exciting movement takes place. Some motor milestones that children reach between 12 and 36 months include:

- *Throwing and kicking a ball (12 months):* Around his first birthday, a child will show increased interest in playing with balls. Initially, he will enjoy throwing a ball. By age two, he will not only like to throw the ball but also kick it. Catching a ball is a more sophisticated skill that may not emerge until age three or four. Help a child with special needs to learn to throw by rolling a small, soft ball back and forth between you and the child, moving farther apart with each pass. Soon, he will understand that he needs to throw the ball to get it to you, and he will enjoy seeing the ball in the air. Laugh and make the activity a fun, interactive game, and stop when the child appears to be getting tired. For kicking, show him how to use his feet instead of his hands to roll a ball back and forth. You could introduce the idea of using his feet to push the ball back to you while he is sitting on the floor. Catching, however, is a more complex task. To help a child with special needs learn to catch a ball, roll the ball down a small incline toward him. This will make it easier for him to practice catching the ball.

Children with visual challenges need extra opportunities to practice new skills.

- *Pushing and pulling (12 to 18 months):* Once a child becomes mobile, he becomes more confident in his ability to stay upright and he may start to drag or push a toy along. For children with special needs, look for toys he can push with both hands such as a toy lawn mower or a favorite doll in a stroller.
- *Squatting (12 to 18 months):* Prior to this age, a child has usually picked objects up from the ground by bending down to get them. Now, he begins an attempt to squat down to pick things up. Demonstrate

this movement by showing a child with special needs how to bend his knees. Playing games that require bending and standing up repeatedly also allows him to learn to use squatting movements. Some simple things you can do include lining up a few objects on the floor and inviting the child to pick up his favorite one. You can then combine both bending and squatting into one similar game and have the child practice following simple commands. For example, instruct the child to bend and pick up a specific item and then to squat and pick up another item.

- *Climbing (12 to 24 months):* Once a child learns to climb, he will follow his natural tendency to explore. Often, toddlers and two-year-olds attempt to climb up a bookshelf, on top of a table, or onto a ledge just because it is there. Children at this age often see these activities as challenging without an understanding of the risk involved. This is especially true of children with special needs. Climbing is an important physical milestone; you should provide developmentally appropriate equipment designed for young climbers. For children with special needs, work closely with a physical therapist or occupational therapist who can recommend adaptive climbing equipment, such as climbing structures with extra hand holds or railings for the child to hold onto when climbing.

- *Running (18 to 24 months):* During this period, some children seems to go from crawling to running overnight while others take more time. Children often stumble and fall when learning to run; some are more willing to risk falling than others. Those with special needs may be reluctant to run because they are not as sure of their balance. You should not force a child to run if he is not ready. While the rest of the class is playing a game that requires running, the child with special needs may also be able to participate. Instead of running, he may prefer to walk fast. For the child who is just starting to experiment with running, it may help if you hold his hand or encourage him to run into your arms.

- *Jumping (24 to 36 months):* Between two and three years of age, children learn how to jump off low structures and, eventually, how to jump from a standing position. Both skills require **bilateral coordination**, the ability to use both sides of the body to do something different. Do not be surprised if a child with special needs delays his attempt to jump until much later. To help the child practice jumping, try holding his hand, stand next to him on a curb or a low step, and say, "One, two, three, jump!" Then, jump together. It is also fun to practice jumping like a bunny or hopping like a frog.

Toilet Training

Toilet training is one of the milestones parents and teachers look forward to the most—no more diapers! But, keep in mind that the age at which a particular child is ready for toilet training varies widely, ranging from 18 to 36 months. For children with special needs, it often takes longer and can be as late as age five or six before they are ready to start toilet training. Because each child is unique, it is hard to know exactly when to start toilet training a particular child. Here are some suggestions that may help determine when a child with special needs is ready to begin toilet training. Regardless, it is important to realize that even after a child is toilet trained, accidents can and do still happen. It may be time to begin toilet training if a child does the following:

- Exhibits the ability to follow simple instructions;
- Indicates discomfort with dirty diapers and wants them to be changed;
- Pulls down his diaper, grabs it, or attempts to pull it off when it is soiled;
- Recognizes when he has a full bladder or needs to have a bowel movement;
- Squats or crosses his legs when he needs to go to the bathroom;
- Shows an interest in things that are related to toilet training, such as wanting to observe others going to the bathroom or talking about going "pee-pee" or "poo-poo";
- Uses a sign or gesture that indicates he needs to urinate or have a bowel movement; or
- Asks to use the bathroom (speech, sign, gesture, or pointing to a picture) or asks to wear regular underwear.

Actions like these indicate he is likely mature enough to understand how his body works. It may be time to give toilet training a try when a child can get himself on and off the toilet and is able to pull his pants down. Help him associate the "about-to-go" sensation with using the toilet. For example, if the child is squirming or pulling at his pants, say, "Let's use the potty!" as you guide him toward it. More suggestions for how to toilet train a child with special needs can be found in Chapter 5.

The Behavior of Toddlers and Twos

A new sense of autonomy, resulting from improved locomotion, also brings with it a new sense of ownership. To a toddler or a two-year-old, the world and everything in it is his. If that is not enough, he is also fully convinced that the entire world and all its inhabitants are there to serve his needs! This egocentric stage is characterized by his lack of understanding that this world view is impossible.

As a result of their egocentric attitudes, toddlers and two-year-olds are prone to tantrums and outbursts designed to indicate their displeasure. It is difficult to separate a tantrum by a typical two-year-old from a tantrum by a two-year-old with special needs. If possible, determine the function or cause of a tantrum. In typically developing children, a tantrum may result from the child's inability to express himself, a reaction to too much stress, a lack of sleep, or the child's failure to get what he wants. The same reasons apply to children with special needs. In addition, their frustration may be increased by a lack of intellectual ability or

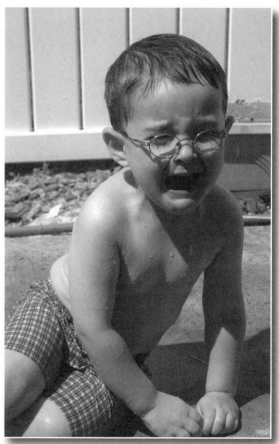

Crying can be an early form of communication.

communication skills necessary for expression. To help a child with special needs avoid having a tantrum, try the following:

- Teach the child to use a gesture or sign to indicate when he is upset or wants something.
- Provide a place where the child can go to be quiet when the activity around him becomes overwhelming. This "quiet area" should have soft lighting and comfortable seating.
- Learn to identify specific warning signs that a child is getting frustrated or upset and redirect his attention before an outburst occurs.

Social Development

Social development is critical during the period of late infancy to age three. As the young child interacts more with others, he soon learns more complex social behaviors and becomes increasingly aware that he can initiate interactions with others. As the child becomes more goal-directed, he may develop motivation toward these interactions. In the literature, this is referred to as **social mastery** or **social motivation**, which may be extremely difficult for children with special needs. For example, a child who is medically fragile or chronically ill may be limited in the kinds of social interactions he experiences. As a result, his social motivation may be less direct than that of his peers.

Children learn social skills by watching others. For example, if a child observes that other children do not want to sit by him when he behaves a certain way, he may seek to change his behavior so others will want to be near him. Children with special needs, especially those with cognitive challenges, often require more direct instruction before they learn how to change or modify an unacceptable behavior. This can happen because the child with cognitive challenges may not be able to connect his behavior with the fact that his peers do not want to sit by him. Additional attention or direction from you will help him better understand the behaviors that lead to better interactions.

Enjoying time alone is a skill that helps children develop independence.

Why Are Social Skills Important?

In essence, social skills are the fundamental skills necessary to get along with others. The time during which social skills are developed is also the time when young children learn how to make friends, how to treat other people, and how to interact socially. Because most toddlers and two-year-olds function in the egocentric stage of "me, it's mine, it's all about me," collaboration does not fully develop until much later, when they interact and learn to collaborate with their peers. Most children with special needs have considerable difficulty behaving appropriately in social situations because they often do not have the skills needed to watch what others are doing and imitate their action or behavior. Children with special needs, especially those with autism spectrum disorder, struggle with social cues and are frequently unable to establish lasting social relationships. A discussion of what can be done to help children with special needs develop social skills can be found in Chapter 8.

Social development relies on many factors. For example, the amount of contact a toddler or two-year-old has with other children, as well as the presence or absence of siblings in the home, are both contributing factors in a child's ability to interact socially. In general, social development occurs in conjunction with cognitive and emotional development, and, as a toddler matures, his social relationships become more complex. The average 24- to 36-month-old will demonstrate some or all of these social characteristics:

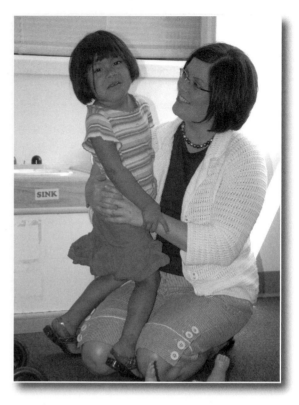

Behavior issues often require direct intervention.

- Plays alone;
- Is self-absorbed, but willing to interact if the activity is of interest to him;
- Depends on adults for guidance;
- Uses socialization as a means to get something he wants or needs;
- Has a limited understanding of the feelings or needs of others; and
- Demonstrates some difficulty when he is over-stimulated by the environment.

Separation Anxiety

Separation anxiety, or fear of a parent leaving, is a common characteristic in young children. Fortunately, it is usually only a phase that most children outgrow by age three. In some cases, however, it is more than a phase and can develop into chronic separation anxiety that can be manifested in physical signs, such as vomiting or headache. One or more of the following are "typical" separation anxiety characteristics in older infants, toddlers, and two-year-olds:

- Persistent, unrealistic fear that some destructive event will happen, preventing the return of the adult.
- Belief that something will happen to increase the time of separation from the adult.
- Unwillingness to go to sleep without the adult's presence.
- Fear of being left alone.
- Repeated signs of distress, including tantrums, crying, and pleading for the adult to stay.
- Repeated need to talk to or call out to the adult.

As with most children, those with special needs will ordinarily have some degree of separation anxiety, while the condition appears stronger and lasts longer in children who are overly dependent on their parents and those whose special needs limit their mobility and activity levels. The following suggestions should help ease the anxiety of children with special needs:

- Help the child feel safe and reassured that the adult will return, but do not dwell on the subject. If the child repeatedly asks when mommy or daddy will be back, try to redirect him to a fun activity or game.
- Help the child develop social skills to cope with being left by the parent. If he feels more confident, he may be less anxious.
- Encourage routines that help the child feel secure, such as having a "Morning Welcome Time." Remember to address the child by name when he arrives at school.
- If the child gets upset and screams or cries, make sure he has time to transition to his new surroundings and circumstances and time to calm down before directing him to an activity.

Communication

Between 12 and 18 months, infants begin to use words and gestures to communicate. This is also when they begin to understand more about how language is used by others. Research has shown that children understand language long before they actually learn to use it. Some children may even be able to use **metacommunication**, which means they begin to communicate about their relationships with others and may communicate differently with different people and in different situations.

As children begin to realize that everything has a name, which usually occurs somewhere between 18 and 24 months, a vocabulary spurt is typically observed. Infants and younger toddlers also start to combine words at this age and will begin to use communication for multiple reasons. This is when some children start speaking in more than just two-word phrases and may attempt to describe a simple activity. As children continue to practice verbal communication, and subsequently become more adept at using it, they begin to ask questions for the purpose of getting information. "Why?" is certainly the question they ask most frequently.

Between 24 and 36 months, simple grammatical usage emerges, as children begin to use verbs more frequently. In addition, they add appropriate endings to words, allowing for the application of tense and number. While variable, it is estimated that a typically developing three-year-old has a vocabulary of about 350 words, which is a tremendous leap from the 50 he knew a few months earlier.

Cognitive Development

Older infants develop increasingly complex ways to solve problems using trial and error. Novel experiences provide a great opportunity to fine-tune problem-solving skills. As they develop cognitively, the average 12- to 18-month-old begins to understand that things belong in categories. For example, they can see that all animals belong to one general category, vehicles fall under another category, and so on. As they continue to mature, they learn to solve problems with less trial-and-error investigation, and, by age two, most infants are pretty adept at solving problems. By 24 months of age, children also use **symbolic play**, which means they use one item to represent another, as when Alex picks up a block, looks at another child, says "Smile!," and uses the block to pretend to take a picture of his peer.

Provide visual clues to help children learn new concepts.

In addition, as children continue to grow and mature, their cognitive processes develop. By age three, most children have a longer attention span, can categorize thoughts and memories into sequences, and can verbally narrate a past experience. This **autobiographical memory** is believed by some to indicate high-level thinking and processing skills. Children soon learn to follow three-step commands and can build on past knowledge to solve new and more complex problems.

Literacy

It is never too soon to begin reading to a child. In fact, reading and talking to a young child have been shown to be predictors of future reading success. Suggestions to help build all children's pre-literacy skills include the following:

- Select books that are of interest to the child and read with them often.
- Provide picture books and board books for the children to explore.

Reading to children builds early literacy skills.

- Build phonological awareness by helping children see and use the sounds in words.
- Play games and sing songs that develop oral language and listening skills.

Toddlers, Twos, and Humor

Many researchers believe humor is the key to social, emotional, and cognitive development. Some have even gone so far as to state that humor is as important to emotional well-being as eating and nutrition are to physical well-being. As a child begins to understand language, verbal humor is a great source of amusement. Rhymes, silly names, nonsense words, and funny games help build an understanding of humor. Many toddlers and two-year-olds enjoy listening to you sing a song or say a funny poem repeatedly. Children this age can also anticipate humor. For example, if you repeat specific jokes, the child will giggle before the punch line. Often, he will join in and sing with you or ask for the song to be repeated. To help a child develop his sense of humor, remember to be playful and willing to laugh. Because toddlers and two-year-olds are, by nature, very physical, one of the best ways to make a child laugh is to chase him and pretend to be unable to catch him. Sudden noises or movements may get laughs as well, but it is important to note that many children, especially those with special needs, are easily frightened by sudden movements or loud noises. Here are some games that include humor and reinforce interaction and that can easily be adapted for children with special needs:

- *Peek-a-boo variations* include encouraging the child to "hide" under a scarf or blanket while you "search" for him, or covering your face halfway when you play the game. You can also build on one of the ideas behind peek-a-boo, which is to teach body parts. For example, cover your left hand with a scarf, wiggle your fingers under the scarf, and say, "Where are my fingers?" See if the child will lift the scarf to find them.
- *Ring Around the Rosey.* Play this game the traditional way if the child is able. If not, look for ways in which he can **partially participate**. One way may be walking along with him and helping him "fall down" by lowering him with your arms. Try variations, such as "all run around," "jump up and down," or "touch the ground."
- *Old MacDonald Had a Farm.* Once a child knows animal sounds, what could be more fun than substituting a child's name for an animal, such as, "On his farm he had a Brandon, e-i-e-i-o," and so on.
- *Rhyme Time.* Young children love rhyming sounds, especially funny rhyming names. Use a child's name to make up nonsensical chants, and encourage the child to follow along and make up his own rhymes.
- *Mirror, Mirror on the Wall!* Sit with the child in front of a mirror. Make a funny face, wait, and see if the child will attempt to imitate you or maybe even make a funny face of his own!

Summary

- A toddler's newly developed motor skills (like walking, running, and climbing) provide opportunities for exploration and cognitive development as he learns new ways to solve problems.
- A child's new awareness of the consequences of being more independent can result in bouts of separation anxiety, as well as internal conflicts between a desire to explore and a desire to be near those he is most comfortable with.
- Developmental milestones for toddlers and two-year-olds vary widely. Keep in mind that a child born prematurely may reach milestones slightly later than a child who was born full-term. By age two, both the premature child and the full-term child will even out developmentally.
- Signs that a developmental delay is more than just a "lag" in development will become more apparent during the toddler months. Other than several delayed milestone achievements, signs that should alert a teacher include the toddler's frequent irritability, the fact that he seldom smiles, makes few or no sounds, and shows no interest in exploration or interaction with others.
- As hand-eye coordination improves (usually around age two), most toddlers and two-year-olds enjoy doing puzzles, playing with blocks, scribbling, and drawing.
- By age three, language skills develop rapidly and vocabulary increases dramatically. Reciting nursery rhymes, singing songs, and reading books are especially fun and appropriate activities for a child this age.

Terms Used in This Chapter

autobiographical memory—Recalling a specific event or activity that occurred in the past.

bilateral coordination—The ability to use both sides of one's body to do something different, such as walking or running.

daily schedule picture cards—Individual cards with pictures that are used to provide clues or cues about the daily schedule.

generalize—Applying previously learned information to a new situation.

metacommunication—A complex form of communication. Examples include talking about relationships with others and changing the type of communication used to fit different contexts.

partial participation —The concept that if a child is unable due to challenges or limitations to fully participate in an activity then he participates as much as he is able.

picture sequence cards—Cards that are placed in order to depict the sequence in which an activity is completed.

social mastery or **social motivation**—Term used to describe behaviors which indicate the child has mastered a specific behavior needed for social interaction.

successive approximation or **shaping**—A technique used for encouragement in which a child receives praise for close approximation to the correct answer or action.

symbolic play—A type of play in which one item becomes a symbol for another such as picking up a block and pretending it is a camera.

Resources Used in This Chapter

Blasco, P. M. (2001). *Early intervention services for infants, toddlers, and their families.* Needham Heights, MA: Allyn & Bacon.

Fogel, A. (2001). *Infancy: Infant, family and society.* Belmont, CA: Wadsworth Learning.

Puckett, M. B., & Black, J. K. (2007). *Understanding toddler development.* St. Paul, MN: Redleaf Press.

Reiff, M. I., & Macias, M. M. (October, 2006). Infant/toddler social-emotional and behavior problems. *Journal of Developmental & Behavioral Pediatrics, 27*(5), 425.

For More Information

Keenan, H. T., Runyan, D. K., & Nocera, M. (2006). Longitudinal follow-up of families and young children with traumatic brain injury. *Pediatrics, 117*(4), 1291–1297.

Laible, D., Panfile, T., & Makariev, D. (2008). The quality and frequency of mother-toddler conflict: Links with attachment and temperament (Report). *Child Development, 79*(2), 426–444.

Matthews, D., Lieven, E., & Tomasello, M. (2007). How toddlers and preschoolers learn to uniquely identify referents for others: A training study. *Child Development, 78*(6), 1744–1759.

Naber, F. B. A., Swinkels, S. H. N., Buitelaar, J. K., Dietz, C., van Daalen, E., Bakermans-Kranenburg, M. J., et al. (2007). Joint attention and attachment in toddlers with autism. *Journal of Abnormal Child Psychology, 35*(6), 899–911.

Specker, B. (2004). Nutrition influences bone development from infancy through toddler years. *The Journal of Nutrition, 134*(3), 691S-695S.

Turati, C., Bulf, H., & Simion, F. (2008). Newborns' face recognition over changes in viewpoint. *Cognition, 106*(3), 1300-1321.

Wetherby, A. M., Woods, J., Allen, L., Cleary, J., Dickinson, H., & Lord, C. (2004). Early Indicators of Autism Spectrum Disorders in the Second Year of Life. *Journal of Autism and Developmental Disorders, 34*(5), 473–493.

Environments for Infants, Toddlers, and Twos

4

Provide assistance while still encouraging peer-to-peer interaction.

Preparation Before the Child Arrives

The best way to prepare for a child with special needs is to learn as much as possible about the child before she comes into your classroom. Encourage the child and her family to visit your class before the first day of school when other children are not present. This initial visit gives you time to get to know the child and gives her time to become familiar with your classroom. Most preschools have a parent information form. However, you should try to find out more about the child than what is included on the form. These are some important questions to ask before a child joins your classroom:

- What does she like to eat? Are there certain foods that she will not eat or that will cause her to react in a certain way?
- What particular interests does she have? Does she have an attachment to a particular toy or object?

Note

The first time a term is used in this chapter it appears in bold. All terms in bold are defined at the end of this chapter, beginning on page 59.

- Does she have a specific song or activity that she enjoys?
- How does she communicate with others?
- What might cause her to become upset or frustrated?
- What does her family think are her strengths?
- What does her family think are her challenges?
- Who is her pediatrician?
- What other services does she receive? Speech therapy? Occupational therapy?
- Are there other children at home?
- How does her family handle issues specifically related to her special need?
- How much experience has she had with other children?

Setting the Stage for Success

Although the environment is crucial to the development of all children, it is even more important for a child with special needs. A space that is too confining can limit a child's natural desire to explore. Also, a lack of materials and supplies can cause young children to interact with each other in ways that are not only unproductive, but detrimental to developing social skills. If the child uses specialized equipment, such as a walker or wheelchair, the open spaces in the classroom must be wide enough to accommodate the equipment and materials need to be placed where the child can access them from the walker or wheelchair. To help optimize development across all domains, there are several aspects of the environment that you must consider. For instance:

- Arrange the physical space to ensure that the environment is accessible by all children.
- Follow a daily schedule that promotes optimal activity and development, while keeping in mind the unique needs of a child or children with special needs.
- Set up activity areas and learning centers that encourage learning, along with play and exploration.
- Promote the children's independence.
- Provide appropriate and adaptable materials that enable children to learn important problem-solving skills.
- Promote positive interactions and the development of social skills.

Provide center-time activities that encourage learning new concepts.

Why Is the Environment so Important?

For young children's optimal learning and development, they need a well-planned, appropriately adapted environment that provides a favorable atmosphere for all of the children's experiences and interactions. In other words, it sets the stage for learning and development across all domains. An optimal environment for all infants, toddlers, and two-year-olds, especially those with special needs, must enable children to acquire and use new skills and to generalize those skills. This is essential to children's ability to adapt to various settings, participate in activities, and interact with others. An optimal learning environment is also essential to nurturing children's emotional and psychological well-being.

If instruction is intentional and planned and allows adequate time for a child to practice and learn a new skill before another is introduced, a child is more likely to acquire new skills. To facilitate a child's learning and development you must not only understand her needs, but must also be aware of her interests. It is critical that the adults in her life work together to plan which skills to teach first and provide the best opportunities for her to practice those skills in various environments. For example, Tara is nine months old. She has developmental delays, especially in the areas of motor skills and communication. If you work with her on the activity of bringing her hands to mid-line while holding a object, and that skill is not reinforced or practiced at home, it will take Tara much longer to learn that skill and make it part of her repertoire.

Structure the environment so children can practice newly acquired skills.

Skill facilitation, another key environmental factor, gives the child an opportunity to practice and use a skill she has already learned. The surroundings should be structured or adapted in such a way that it increases the likelihood that the skill will be used. Research has shown that skill acquisition and facilitation is more likely to take place in the **natural environment** than it is to occur in an artificial one. The natural environment refers to a place or setting where typically developing children would most likely have the opportunity or need to use a particular skill. For example, if the goal for the child is to bring a spoon to her mouth and attempt to feed herself, she should practice that skill while she is eating (the natural environment), not while sitting alone at a table and repeatedly bringing an empty spoon to her mouth to practice the skill (an artificial environment). It is important that the child is able to associate the action of bringing the spoon to her mouth with actually eating food.

As discussed in Chapter 3, the ability to generalize (transfer a skill learned in one context to another setting, person, or object) is often very difficult for children with special needs. For example, Talisha can stack two blocks in the block area of the classroom. She does this by picking up one block, and, using both hands, places it on top of another block. However, she cannot stack two similar blocks at home. Also, when asked to stack two items other than blocks in the block area, she looks to her teacher for help. Talisha has learned to stack the two blocks in one context or setting but has not learned that the same skill she uses to stack the blocks at school can be used in other settings and with other materials. In other words, she is unable to generalize these activities.

An important aspect of a supportive environment is that it nurtures the children. Nurturing environments are places where children feel loved and safe to explore and learn. According to David and Weinstein (1987), environments should fulfill five basic functions for young children, including:

1. Foster personal identity and a sense of belonging.
2. Enable children to develop confidence and master new skills.
3. Provide opportunities for growth in stimulating surroundings.
4. Encourage a sense of security and trust by being safe, warm, inviting, and predictable.
5. Be designed so that children have opportunities for both social interaction and privacy.

Mirrors can help children learn new skills.

Arranging the Physical Space for Accessibility by All Children

When considering accessibility, there is a tendency to focus on things like ramps for the child in a wheelchair or materials that have been adapted for a child with special needs. Accessibility, however, goes beyond just meeting a child's physical needs. It also includes meeting the child's communication, emotional, cognitive, and social needs, across all domains. A responsive environment for infants, toddlers, and two-year-olds with special needs includes the following:

- *Materials designed to be challenging and provide feedback.* In other words, offer materials that allow adequate difficulty to challenge the child without setting her up for failure. Do not give her something that requires too much physical or mental effort for her ability. For example, most infants enjoy a toy that, when touched or squashed will light up or make a noise. The same may be true for a child with special needs, but if she does not understand how to activate the toy, she will get frustrated and give up.
- *Adults who know how to read non-verbal communication signs.* For example, Tabitha is a 15-month-old with vision loss. It is important while feeding her to allow her to smell the food on the spoon before she puts it in her mouth. If, after a few bites, she begins to lean forward toward the spoon, you could say, "Oh, Tabitha, you want more applesauce." By doing this, you are letting Tabitha know that you understand her non-verbal request for more food.
- *A physical setting that is not too crowded or overwhelming.* The child should have adequate space to move around the area and be able to access the materials or objects that she wants and needs. Remember also that there should be ample opportunity for her to use these materials. Another example of facilitating the environment may include making sure appropriate furniture is available, so that all children can be accommodated. For example, for many toddlers and two-year-olds with special needs, child-sized chairs are too uncomfortable or difficult to use. Try using alternatives, like large, comfortable pillows or beanbag chairs.

The Daily Schedule for Infants

Planning a daily schedule for infants with special needs can be challenging. It is vital to meet with the infant's family so you can determine which times are best for her to eat, play, and rest. Some infants with special needs require more rest than their peers. However, each child is unique and will ultimately have her own preferences and needs. It is also important to know as much as possible about the infant's special needs. For example, a child with cerebral palsy will require specific feeding techniques once baby food is introduced, and an infant with Down syndrome who also has heart defects will require periods of rest during feeding time. Infants with **Bronchopulmonary Dysplasia (BPD)**, a condition occurring in some premature infants that results in sensitive, immature lungs that are easily inflamed, will require more frequent bottle feeding to prevent dehydration.

When arranging a daily schedule for infants with special needs, it is important to allow as much flexibility as possible. In general, these aspects should be considered:

- Most infants are more alert in the morning.
- There should be multiple times during the day allotted for active play, rest, eating, and quiet play.
- Feeding an infant with special needs may take longer than usual.
- While some infants with special needs require more rest and sleep than their peers, some require less.
- Consideration must be given for the child's therapies, such as speech, language, physical therapy, or occupational therapy.

Arrival Time

Arrival time may be the most important time of the day for a toddler or two-year-old. The child's manner and temperament when she arrives in the classroom may set the tone of her mood all day. Separation anxiety (discussed in Chapter 3) is common for many children and happens frequently when the parent leaves the room. However, there are methods that may help the reluctant toddler or two-year-old with special needs deal with separation anxiety:

- Greet the child the same way each day.
- Lean or squat down so you are at eye level with her, and remember to call her by name.
- Keep in mind that a child with special needs, especially a child with sensory impairments, may respond better if you gently touch her on the arm or shoulder when you address her.
- Try using music to help the child transition to your classroom. Try the following "Welcome Song" to help with transitions.

  Welcome Song by Clarissa Willis
  Tune: "Three Blind Mice"

  Hello, (insert child's name),
  Hello, (insert child's name),
  I'm glad you're here! I'm glad you're here!
  Let's put your things away and find out what to do today,
  Hello, (insert child's name),
  Hello, (insert child's name).

- Some children with special needs may need extra cues to help them understand what is expected of them. Try using a communication apron (apron with pictures attached) or a picture schedule to show the child what to do when she arrives.

While a schedule for a toddler or two-year-old is usually more structured than an infant schedule, it is still important to keep in mind that children with special needs may need more flexibility, especially with respect to the times when they need to eat or rest. Most daily schedules include:

- Large group time (usually two or more per day);
- Small group time;

- Individual instruction;
- Free-choice time (usually spent in learning centers);
- Creative activities (art, music, drama, and so on);
- Transitions between activities; and
- Time for active play and climbing, either outdoors or indoors.

Let's look at each one and see how they can be adapted for children with special needs.

Large Group Time

Whether it is called "circle time" or "large group time," this important time is when the entire class is involved in a single activity. It is also the most challenging time for children with special needs (Isbell & Isbell, 2005). This is especially true for children with autism, behavior challenges, and those with extremely short attention spans, which describes almost every young child. To make this time meaningful for toddlers and young children with special needs, remember to keep it short (less than five minutes) and follow these guidelines:

- Plan activities that require participation by the whole class. If the activity can be adapted for a small group, which is preferable, do it! Because toddlers and two-year-olds vary greatly in their development and interest levels, whole group instruction is far less effective than small group and individual instruction.
- Keep large group time as short as possible. For a child with significant issues, sitting through a large group activity may be impossible. Consider allowing the child to participate for a minute, at first, and gradually increase her participation time. Keep in mind that many toddlers and two-year-olds are simply unable to sit comfortably in a large group.
- Make the activity as meaningful as possible for the child with special needs. This may involve giving her props to use during the activity. For example, the use of puppets often works well. Plan multi-sensory activities, such as passing around objects of different shapes, textures, or sizes.
- Incorporate movement and music during large group instruction. Children are more likely to participate if they are actively doing something, rather than just sitting and listening.
- Make sure the seating is comfortable. Scratchy carpet squares are not practical for young children. If the activity involves sitting, use alternatives like beanbag chairs, pillows, and soft blankets.

Large group time should include interactive fingerplay games.

- Consider making large group time optional. Some toddlers and two-year-olds can tolerate sitting in a group with other children. Others, especially those who are developmentally delayed, are just not yet ready to participate in such a setting.

Small Group Time

Small group time usually involves working with only a few children. If possible, keep the group size to four or less, especially if children with special needs are in the group. It is during small group time that more individualized and intentional instruction takes place. Be sure you are familiar with the child's **IFSP** or **IEP**, so you know which goals need work and how to plan opportunities for the child to practice previously acquired skills. Select groups based on **temperament** as well as ability level. Below are some guidelines for helping a child with special needs function in a small group.

- Review what was previously learned, keeping in mind that after a long break, such as after a holiday or long weekend, the children may need extra review.
- Remember that a child with special needs may have trouble generalizing information; provide as many concrete examples as possible.
- Provide multiple opportunities for participation. Ask questions frequently and look for ways to keep the child engaged. If she is non-verbal, look for ways to help her be part of the group.
- Offer the child opportunities to practice.
- The child may need extra time to process new information, so plan accordingly.
- Provide positive feedback, and don't forget to praise a child for her attempts, even if those attempts are not successful.

Individual Instruction

Individualized instruction time is when you or another adult works one on one with the child. This instruction should always be intentional and meaningful. It is during this time that the child may receive additional instruction from a speech-language pathologist, an occupational therapist, or an early interventionist. It is very important that you inform the child's family about her progress, and make sure to encourage the family to reinforce at home what you are working on at school.

Free Choice Time

Free choice time is the child-initiated portion of the day, when children have a choice about what they do and where they do it. In a classroom, free choice time is usually spent in learning centers or in working with one or more peers in a specific area, such as the block center, climbing area, dress-up center, and so on. Some suggestions of modifications of learning centers for toddlers or two-year-olds with special needs in traditional and a few non-traditional learning centers are provided in Table 4–1.

Table 4–1 *Modifications for Learning Centers*

Center	Modifications
Literacy	• Include books that feature people with disabilities who are part of the community. • Offer plenty of large "board books" that have bright pictures. • Provide books that make noise when they are opened or have different textures that a child can touch, such as in *Pat the Bunny*. • Children with motor delays may need adaptive equipment, such as a "page-turner," to help them turn pages or a special switch to help them turn a tape recorder on and off.
Block	• Offer blocks of different sizes and other materials that can be stacked, such as clean plastic food containers or boxes. • Consider using blocks with handles or knobs so a child with motor delays can participate in building activities.
Manipulatives	• Provide puzzles with knobs and handles. • Offer activities that help develop fine motor skills, such as the Fisher-Price Rock 'n Stack Baby or the Fisher-Price Activity Center™.
Exploration	• Offer magnifying glasses of varying strengths. If possible, provide one that has a built-in light. • Provide large and small items to explore. • Add a pair of tongs to help children with fine motor issues pick up objects.
Music	• Provide opportunities to dance, sing, and play music on instruments. • Adapt tape recorders with switches so that children can turn them on and off more easily.
Art	• Provide adaptive paintbrushes and double-hold scissors for children with motor issues. • Include art materials in bright colors. • Provide materials in a variety of textures and media (clay, paint, paper, sand, and so on) to encourage exploration of new things.
Computer	• Make sure there is an adaptive keyboard, such as Intellikeys™ (see page 152 in the Appendix—Adaptive Equipment), available for children with special needs. • Provide computer programs for varying abilities and skills. Programs that offer instant feedback are especially good for children with special needs.
Quiet	• Make sure there are comfortable places to sit and the lighting is soft. • Provide an audio player with headphones so the child can listen to music. If necessary, fit the player with an adaptive switch or battery interrupter so the child can turn it on and off.
Dress-Up	• Place clothes in the dress-up center that have buttons and zippers to give the child extra practice. • Provide clothes of varying colors, and invite the child to sort them by color, shape, size, and other attributes. • Include hats, caps, and accessories, such as shoes and purses.

(Continued)

Table 4–1 *Modifications for Learning Centers (continued)*

Center	Modifications
Home Living	• Make sure some of the materials have large handles for the child to grip. • Home living is a great center for role-play. For example, children can role-play enjoying meals with friends or everyday routines, such as getting ready for bed or preparing for school. • Place sequence cards for everyday things, such as setting the table or getting ready for school, in the center. The cards will help the children learn the steps of routine activities.
Non-Traditional Centers	
Touch	• Provide objects and materials of varying shapes, textures, and sizes. • Make "feely" boxes with things of different textures hidden inside. Remember, some children may be hesitant to put their hands into a box when they cannot see its contents. Offer to do the activity with the child.
Friendship	• This center can reinforce in-class activities by giving children an opportunity to practice friendship skills. • Role-playing activities or friendship circles (a circle where friends sit and talk) are all useful, and can help children with special needs interact with their peers. • Include activities that children can do together, such as building with blocks or painting a mural.
International	• Feature people and places that are new to the children or different from what they are used to. Provide props to go with each activity. This center will help teach about diversity. • Bring foods from other cultures for the children to sample to help them learn about new and different tastes. This is also a good center for collaborative activities.

Transitions Between Activities

Transitions between activities can be especially problematic for children with special needs. The following are a few strategies that you can use to make transitions go more smoothly:

- Let the child know *before* it is time to transition. This can be accomplished by showing her a timer; giving her a specified cue, such as a tap on the shoulder; or by simply telling her it is almost time to transition.
- Make transitions fun. Invite the children to fly like birds, walk like elephants (arms can swing in front for the trunk), gallop like ponies, or tiptoe like mice.

- Use transition helpers, such as music or sound. A song played or sung at each transition can be a great cue that it is time to transition. A xylophone, chime, or a small tinkling bell can also help. Avoid loud noises, such as a large bell or gong, as these are especially difficult for young children with sensory integration issues.

Activities for Infants, Toddlers, and Twos with Special Needs

- *Contingency response needs*: Infants with special needs will need to learn how their movements affect their surroundings or how they can cause environmental reaction. In other words, the primary goal for many infants with special needs is to learn cause and effect. One way to begin teaching this is to tie a piece of yarn around an infant's foot and attach the other end to a mobile, bell, or toy that can be activated by movement. When the infant moves her legs, the item moves. **Note**: Supervise closely. Another way to accomplish this is to sit with the infant in your lap and guide her hands toward a ball. Help her push the ball forward and watch it roll away.
- *Consider the unique learning needs of each child*: For example, a visually impaired infant will need activities that have a sound component, while a child with hearing loss will respond better to something bright and colorful. In addition, a child with motor delays will need materials that are easily reached and easy to pick up.
- *Plan activities based on your knowledge of the child's ability*: Careful observation can show when a young child is ready to learn something. For example, when you observe an infant trying to bring her hands to the mid-line, plan activities to help her reinforce that skill. Or, if you see a toddler playing with blocks, plan activities to help her learn to stack the blocks.

Techniques to Help Infants, Toddlers, and Twos Learn a New Skill

Techniques that make activities more meaningful for young children with special needs include:

- **Successive approximation** or **shaping** is a technique that supports a child as she attempts a task. When a child is trying to learn a new activity or work on solving a problem that may be difficult for her, it helps to reinforce her efforts with praise for close approximations. This praise, or "reward," encourages her to continue trying to achieve a new goal.
- Modeling is often necessary to help a toddler or two-year-old understand how to complete a task. With modeling, there is always an expectation that the

learner can copy the model. When modeling a new task or activity for a child with special needs, it is very helpful if you break down the task into smaller steps and invite the child to repeat each step after it is demonstrated.

- **Cueing** is a technique that you can use to give the child clues about what she is expected to do. For example, if Kara always runs ahead into a learning center instead of waiting her turn, place your hand on Kara's shoulder to cue her to wait until it is her turn.

Using Observation Skills to Guide Instruction

Direct observation is one of the best methods to use to help you know how to plan activities for young children with special needs. The following guidelines will help you know what to observe and how to document the observations:

- Select a method for recording your observation that is easy to use and convenient. For example, try color-coded index cards, held together by hole-punching the cards and inserting a single ring in the right-hand corner. Use each card to write down your observations and notes about a child. Date the cards and attach them to your belt loop or hang them on a pegboard. Whatever method you use, always put the date and time on each observational note that you make.
- Practice observing what the child says and does, and how she acts. Record exactly what you hear and see, not what you feel. Avoid making broad generalizations, such as, "Richard bites other children." Instead, you should record, "Richard bit Justin when Justin tried to play with a truck that Richard was already playing with."
- Write down your observations as close to the time they occur as possible. It is easy to forget important information if you wait until the end of the school day.
- Describe the context of the child's behavior and actions. For example, you could make a notation, such as, "Alissa left small group today and crawled under the table instead of going to center time."
- While you observe the child, you may see something you want to examine further. For example, if you notice that the child always seems to play more cooperatively before lunch than after, you may want to make a note for yourself to observe her for a few days before lunch to see if this behavior indicates a pattern.
- Try to observe the child in a variety of settings and at different times during the day, as this will give you multiple opportunities to document not only what happens but also when it happens.

Terms Used in This Chapter

Bronchopulmonary Dysplasia (BPD)—A condition that occurs in some premature infants that results in sensitive, immature lungs that are inflamed easily.

communication apron—An apron that has pictures or communication cues attached to it.

cueing—A technique used to give a child a clue or hint about what he is supposed to do or how he is expected to respond.

Individualized Education Plan (IEP)—A plan designed to outline goals and objectives for children with special needs age 3-21 who receive special education services.

Individualized Family Service Plan (IFSP)—A document that outlines the services to be delivered to infants, toddlers, and two-year-olds receiving special education services and their families. This document is required by law and is part of the Individuals With Disabilities Education Act (Part C).

natural environment—The environment in which an activity would normally occur.

picture schedule—A pictorial clue about what is to happen within a daily routine or schedule.

skill facilitation—Techniques designed to provide a child with opportunities to practice and learn previously acquired skills.

successive approximation or **shaping**—Refers to a process where a specific behavior is gradually molded or trained to perform a specific response by reinforcing any responses that come close to the desired response.

temperament—The manner of thinking, behaving, or reacting that is characteristic of a specific person.

Resources Used in This Chapter

Bailey, D. B., & Wolery, M. (1992). *Teaching infants and preschoolers with disabilities.* Upper Saddle River, NJ: Merrill.

David, T. & Weinstein, C. (1987). *Spaces for children.* New York: Plenum Press.

Gould, P., & Sullivan, P. (1999). *The inclusive early childhood classroom.* Beltsville, MD: Gryphon House.

Isbell, R., & Isbell, C. (2005).*The inclusive learning center book for preschool children with special needs.* Beltsville, MD: Gryphon House.

Willis, C. (2006). *Teaching young children with autism spectrum disorder.* Beltsville, MD: Gryphon House.

Willis, C. (2009). *Creating inclusive learning environments for young children: What to do on Monday morning.* Thousand Oaks, CA: Corwin Press.

For More Information

Gallagher, P. A., & Lambert, R. G. (2006). Classroom quality, concentration of children with special needs, and child outcomes in head start. *Exceptional Children*, 73(1), 31–53.

Hanson, M. J., Horn, E., Sandall, S., Beckman, P., Morgan, M., Marquart, J., Barnwell, D., & Chou, H. Y. (2001). After preschool inclusion: children's educational pathways over the early school years. *Exceptional Children*, 68(1), 65.

McCormick, L., Wong, M., & Yogi, L. (2003). Individualization in the inclusive preschool: A planning process. *Childhood Education*, 79(4), 212–218.

Williams, A. E. (2008). Exploring the natural world with infants and toddlers in an urban setting. *Young Children*, 63(1), 22–25.

Life Skills

5

Learning to wash your hands is a necessary skill for all children.

What Are Life Skills?

Self-help or life skills have been given many names—everyday skills, independent living skills, and **functional skills**. Regardless of which term you use, a young child will use these skills throughout his life. They will help him function in daily activities and take care of his daily needs. For infants and toddlers, examples of functional skills include going to the bathroom, eating a meal, dressing for school, brushing teeth, and taking a bath. For an older child, a functional skill might include learning to recognize common environmental cues, such as signs for restrooms, exit signs, and stop signs. As a young adult, functional skills might be learning to access community resources, such as the bank, post office, and grocery store. Regardless of a child's age, functional skills (or life skills) are broadly defined as activities that help a person become as independent as possible.

Note
The first time a term is used in this chapter it appears in bold. All terms in bold are defined at the end of this chapter, beginning on page 69.

Why Are Life Skills Important?

For a variety of reasons, acquiring life skills is essential in order for a child to learn the basic routines required to function in his everyday life. First, life skills help the child gain independence, making him feel more in control of his world. Second, learning to take care of basic needs, such as going to the bathroom, eating, and dressing, helps the child socially by allowing him to do the same activities as his typically developing peers. Most important, life skills help the child develop a sense of accomplishment and the confidence that comes from doing it "all by myself." This intense need for independence is a characteristic often identified with children between the ages of 24 and 36 months.

Most young children learn life skills by watching others, copying what adults and peers do, and following directives from adults. Young children with special needs may need some additional help, because they often do not have the aptitude to imitate what others do without extra practice and very explicit and purposeful directions. Additionally, the steps required to accomplish these all-important skills may need to be broken down into smaller steps, and may require prompts or cues to help remind these children what to do next.

Life skills need to be taught as well as practiced in the context of daily routines. It is also important that this occur in the environment in which the child would use that skill. For example, you would not teach a child to wash his hands while sitting at a table in your classroom. Instead, you would take him to the natural environment, in this case the sink, where washing his hands would normally take place. Likewise, you would not use a small group setting to teach a child the steps involved in feeding himself. Teaching and practicing in an artificial environment is not only a waste of time, but can also confuse the child. Remember, children with special needs learn best when information is presented in a context they can relate to; practicing a skill in a time or place in which that skill would not normally occur is confusing for the child and may slow down his progress in developing that skill. Because the child is busy trying to figure out why something is being practiced in a simulated or "pretend" way, he often fails to concentrate on what you are asking him to do.

Life Skill Categories for Infants, Toddlers, and Twos

- *Feeding* (these skills are discussed at length in Chapter 6—Feeding)
    - Progressing from bottle feeding to simple finger foods
    - Using utensils to eat
    - Simple table rules
    - Social context of meal time

- *Toileting*
    - Recognizing when a diaper change is needed
    - Anticipating the need to go to the bathroom
    - Asking to go to the toilet
    - Taking care of own toilet needs
    - Washing hands after toileting
    - Handling unplanned situations

- *Daily routines*
    - o Brushing teeth
    - o Washing and drying face
    - o Tolerating a bath

- *Dressing*
    - o Getting dressed for school
    - o Preparing to go outside (putting on a coat, mittens, and so on)
    - o Putting on shoes
    - o Taking off clothes

Life Skills for Infants, Toddlers, and Twos with Special Needs

Drinking from a cup is a skill that requires practice.

Because most infants, toddlers, and two-year-olds with special needs require extra help to learn self-help skills, instruction should be intentional and planned. Goals for infants with special needs should include the acquisition of eating and feeding skills. For toddlers and two-year-olds, goals may include the understanding and mastery of routines, such as toileting and dressing. It is worth noting again the importance of working with the child's family to achieve these goals, so that the child is encouraged to practice these skills at home as well as at school. For example, when a specific life skill (such as washing hands) is taught, that activity should be reinforced both at home and at school, using the same words and procedures. In addition, it is important for home and school to use the same sequence to teach a child how to function independently within those routines, and to find many opportunities for the child to practice the newly learned skill.

Because most self-help skills build on those skills a child has previously learned, it is critical to know which pre-requisite proficiencies are needed before a child can learn a specific skill. For example, before a toddler tries to dress himself, he must be able to cooperate when an adult dresses him by pushing his arm through a sleeve or by standing up while his pants are pulled down. As he matures, he may begin to try some of these activities independently.

Toileting

According to Bailey and Wolery (1992), toileting is a unique skill for three important reasons:

1. It is a major developmental accomplishment that signals a high degree of independence and is a high-priority skill for families and care providers.
2. It has complex physical requirements as well as learned behaviors, such as knowing when and where to release urine and feces.
3. It is unique from other developmental milestones because it is controlled primarily by the child.

In addition, when an older toddler is still wearing a diaper, it can be the one indicator that a child may have special needs. Being the only child in the room still wearing a diaper isolates the child from his peers and can lead to questions from others about why he is still wearing one. Also, some children with special needs will occasionally have "accidents" if they are not taken to the bathroom regularly. In other words, even though they can technically urinate and defecate into a toilet, they may forget unless they are reminded frequently. This is especially true for children with cognitive challenges and other types of special needs, such as Down syndrome. It is very important to note that some children with paralysis or other more severe conditions may never be able to become independently toilet trained. In these cases, it is important to work toward allowing them to have their physical needs met in a private setting without calling attention to the fact that they wear diapers.

For most children, toilet training is a developmental milestone that follows a predictable pattern. Once children are physiologically ready, with persistence and practice, the desire to "use the potty" outweighs their desire to wear a diaper. Even when there are problems in learning to go to the bathroom or signs of toilet training resistance, typically developing children eventually learn to use the toilet. This is also true of children with special needs. However, instead of being toilet trained by age three, it may take longer. It is not uncommon for a child with special needs to be four or five and still not be completely toilet trained.

Signs of physical readiness to begin using the toilet usually occur when a child is somewhere between 18 months and 3 years of age. It is more important to keep in mind the child's developmental level rather than his chronological age when you are considering toilet training. It is also important to remember that toilet training requires a team effort, where the family and other caregivers must follow the same toileting routine and essentially have the same goals if it is to be successful. In essence, toilet training is divided into discretely interrelated areas: intellectual or psychological readiness, and physiological or physical readiness. Signs of intellectual and psychological readiness include the child's being able to:

- Follow simple instructions,
- Cooperate and tolerate the "potty" routine,
- Be uncomfortable with dirty diapers and want them to be changed,

- Recognize when he has a full bladder or needs to have a bowel movement,
- Be able to communicate to an adult when he needs to urinate or have a bowel movement,
- Ask or gesture to use the potty chair, or
- Ask to wear regular or "grown-up" underwear.

Indications that a child with special needs is physically ready to begin toilet training might include:

- Being able to tell when he is about to urinate or have a bowel movement by his facial expressions, posture, or by what he communicates or gestures;
- Staying dry for at least two hours at a time;
- Having regular bowel movements;
- Understanding that when he is placed on the potty or potty chair, something should happen; and
- Being able to help, at least partially, to dress and undress himself.

Children with physical disabilities may also have problems with toilet training that involve learning to get on the potty and getting undressed before using the potty. A special potty chair and other adaptations may be necessary for some children, especially those with muscle issues or cerebral palsy.

Because an important sign of readiness and a motivator to begin toilet training involves being uncomfortable in a dirty diaper, if the child isn't bothered by a soiled or wet diaper, then it may be a good idea to change him into regular underwear or training pants during daytime toilet training. Once you are ready to begin training, it is important to select a potty chair that fits the child. Whenever a child shows signs of needing to urinate or have a bowel movement, take him to the potty chair and communicate to him what you want him to do. For some children, using pictures serves a way to prompt them about what is expected. Make a consistent routine of having him go to the potty, pull down his pants, sit on the potty, and after he is finished, pulling up his pants and washing his hands. This routine should be followed, even if he does not successfully void in the potty chair.

Initially, keep him seated for a few minutes at a time. Do not attempt to coerce him, and be prepared for some resistance. Until he is going in the potty, you may try to empty his dirty diapers into his potty chair to help demonstrate what you want him to do. Remember that, unless the child is cognitively able to connect the two processes, it may be a waste of time. Another important step involved in successfully toilet training children with special needs is using the toilet frequently. This usually includes a scheduled time for going to the bathroom. Keep in mind that for children with special needs this toilet schedule may be much more frequent than with typically developing children. Make going to the toilet a fun time. Show the child a picture of the potty, then say, "Let's go to the potty." Hold the child's hand or sing a little song as you walk him to the bathroom. Follow these general guidelines for teaching toileting skills to children with special needs:

1. After careful observation, decide if the child has the pre-requisite skills needed to begin toilet training.
2. Collect data about how often the child needs a diaper change and the times when he usually needs a diaper change.
3. Learn to identify signs, such as facial gestures, noises, or other cues that he is about to go to the bathroom.
4. Provide opportunities for children to observe others going to the bathroom. For example, if you take two or three children to the bathroom at the same time, invite the child with special needs to go along and give the child a "turn" at sitting on the toilet, even if nothing happens.
5. Begin training while the child is sitting on the toilet.
6. Help the child communicate (signs, gestures, speech, or pointing to a picture) that he needs to go to the bathroom.
7. Teach each skill the child will need in a toileting routine. Keep in mind that some children may be able to partially participate in the process before they are able to complete a step independently.
8. Expect accidents to happen and don't make a crisis out of them when they occur.

Drying your hands is an important functional or life skill.

How Do I Teach a New Routine?

When teaching a new routine it is best to break each part into smaller ones. For an example, see Table 5–1.

Dressing

For a young child, learning to dress independently is an important life skill and signifies yet another level of independence. Certainly there are some pre-requisite skills needed before a child can independently dress and undress himself. The following are some general goals for children with special needs, based on chronological age:

- Infants–12 months old
  o Cooperates with being dressed or undressed
  o Attempts to help put arms in sleeves or holds up arms to be put into sleeves

- 12–24 months old
  o Takes off shoes and socks
  o Attempts to get an article of clothing
  o May lift up leg for putting on pants
  o May pull shirt over head and attempt to put arms in sleeves

Table 5-1 *Steps in a Toileting Routine*

1. Child recognizes a need to go to the bathroom.

2. Child signals or communicates a need to go to the bathroom. This signal may be in the form of a gesture, sign, pointing to a picture card, or a verbal cue.

3. Child gets the attention of an adult and moves toward the bathroom. If the child is not mobile, he may need extra instruction for getting his walker or wheelchair into the bathroom area.

4. Child enters the bathroom, moves toward the toilet or "potty" chair, or gestures or signs for an adult to help him move toward the toilet or potty chair.

5. Child unfastens or attempts to remove clothes before sitting down. Keep in mind that some children with special needs forget this step; it is not uncommon for a child to sit down on a potty with his clothes on and go to the bathroom.

6. Child, with adult help or independently, pushes pants down far enough so he can sit on the toilet.

7. Child is able to maintain balance while sitting on the toilet and sits there until he goes to the bathroom.

8. Child recognizes when he is finished and reaches for toilet paper. (This is a step many children with special needs forget.)

9. Child wipes himself clean or waits for an adult to wipe him before attempting to pull up clothes.

10. Child stands up and flushes toilet.

11. Child attempts to pull up clothes and arrange them before leaving bathroom.

12. Child goes to sink, turns on water, adds soap to hands, washes hands, rinses hands, and then dries hands. It may be necessary to teach them to count or say a favorite rhyme while washing hands, as there is a tendency to quickly put on soap and rinse without thoroughly cleaning hands.

13. Child dries hands and throws away towel before leaving bathroom.

- 24–36 months old
  - Unzips pants
  - Pulls pants down
  - Pulls pants up from ankles
  - Removes coat, hat, mittens
  - Attempts to put on socks and/or shoes (though often not in the correct sequence)

Table 5–2 on the following page outlines some special tips for helping children with specific issues dress themselves and use the toilet independently.

Table 5–2   *Tips for Helping Children Dress and Use the Toilet*

Type of Special Need	Suggestions for Learning to Dress	Suggestions for Toilet Training
Visual impairments	• Research has shown that for children with visual impairments it is best to use the child's body rather than dolls to practice dressing and undressing. • Use clothing that can help the child function more independently, such as pull-over shirts, Velcro closures on shoes, and a keychain attached to a coat zipper for ease in pulling it up.	• For boys, place a brightly colored ring around the toilet to help orient them to the surface. • Teach girls to back up to the toilet until their legs touch the rim. • Orient the child to soap, toilet paper, paper towels, and so on.
Hearing Impairments	• If the child has a profound hearing loss, learn a few signs for clothing such as *pants, blouse, shoes, and socks.* • Demonstrate or use picture cards to show the child exactly what to do during each step of the process.	• Make sure the child can see your face when you give him instructions. • For a child who has a severe hearing loss, it may be necessary for you to learn sign language. The sign for "bathroom" is made by making a fist, placing the thumb between the second and third fingers, and moving the fist up and down.
Autism	• Always tell the child what is going to happen next. • Keep in mind that, because of their unique sensory integration needs, the child may resist putting on clothes that he perceives as too binding or "scratchy." • Children with autism do not deal with abstract concepts. Therefore, it will work better for a child to dress himself than to practice dressing a doll or puppet.	• Use pictures to show the child each step of the process. • Anticipate that children with autism may have additional issues with the bathroom, such as fear of sitting on the toilet, avoidance to touching toilet paper or of wiping themselves, a need to flush repeatedly, and a resistance to change, which may include a resistance to giving up wearing a diaper.
Language Delays	• Make sure the child knows the vocabulary necessary to understand what you are asking him to do. • Provide opportunities for him to practice dressing himself, a doll, or a puppet.	• Make sure the child has a method to tell you when he needs to go to the bathroom, such as a sign or hand signal. • Ask the child questions to determine that he understands what he is expected to accomplish during a toileting routine.
Motor Delays	• If a child is not able to independently dress himself, it is important that he partially participate. For example, he might hold one sock while you put the other one on him.	• It is possible that a child with severe motor delays will never use the bathroom independently. If this is the case, be sure there is a place that is private for his diaper to be changed. It is important to maintain the child's sense of dignity and discourage questions from other children.

Terms Used in This Chapter

functional skills—The life skills that a child uses to take care of his daily needs and function independently.

Resources Used in This Chapter

Bailey, D. B., & Wolery, M. (1992). *Teaching infants and preschoolers with disabilities.* Upper Saddle River, NJ: Prentice-Hall.

Gould, P., & Sullivan, J. (1999). *The inclusive early childhood classroom.* Beltsville, MD: Gryphon House.

Willis, C. (2006). *Teaching young children with autism spectrum disorder.* Beltsville, MD: Gryphon House.

Willis, C. (2009). *Creating inclusive learning environments for young children: What to do on Monday morning.* Thousand Oaks, CA: Corwin Press.

For More Information

Dunst, C.J. & Dempsey, I. (2007). Family-professional partnerships and parenting competence, confidence, and enjoyment. *International Journal of Disability, Development and Education, 54*(3), 305–318.

Schiller, P., & Willis, C. (2008). *Inclusive literacy lessons.* Beltsville, MD: Gryphon House.

Teaching Infants, Toddlers, and Twos with Special Needs

Eating and Feeding Issues

*Adaptive cups facilitate learning
how to drink from a cup.*

Feeding Infants, Toddlers, and Twos with Special Needs

Feeding an infant with special needs can be overwhelming, especially if the child has challenges that interfere with food intake. This chapter addresses some of the general processes involved in feeding. It is very important, however, to work closely with trained professionals, such as a **nutritionist**, **speech-language pathologist**, **occupational therapist**, or **physical therapist** in determining the proper way to feed a specific child. It is also critical to follow any instructions or recommendations from the child's pediatrician in regard to what to feed, when to feed, and any specific types of allergies the child may exhibit.

Note

The first time a term is used in this chapter it appears in bold. All terms in bold are defined at the end of this chapter, beginning on page 82.

The Process of Eating

Although eating is a fundamental necessity for survival, it is also a time when children learn to socialize and respond to others. The process of eating can be broken down into four components:

1. The need for adequate intake of nutrition. This aspect of feeding depends on both the temperament of the child and your attitude, because feeding a child with special needs can be quite time consuming. It is also important to note that sometimes a child's specific special need may interfere with her getting the nutrition she needs to grow and develop.
2. The ability of the child to control the muscles essential for eating, such as sucking, swallowing, chewing, and biting.
3. The ability of the child to learn the skills needed to eventually feed herself and to ultimately have some control over what she eats.
4. Understanding the cultural expectations and "manners" necessary to participate in a routine meal.

Oral Reflexes

In the typically developing infant, oral reflexes (suckle, swallow) become increasingly more coordinated as the child develops. As she learns to use the muscles in her mouth and throat, she becomes more able to control them when needed for sucking, swallowing, and chewing. During the first month of life, an infant's responses are primarily reflexive and help her survive the first few weeks outside the womb. Reflexes commonly seen include:

- **Rooting reflex** (turning toward the source of food),
- Suckle (sucking with the lips) followed by a swallow (often referred to as the suckle and swallow),
- **Gag reflex** (automatic response to anything that comes into contact with the muscles in the back of the tongue),

The rooting reflex diminishes with time and is gone by 3 to 4 months of age in most infants. Suckle and swallow reflexes are characterized by the tongue moving rhythmically forwards and backwards. Initially, this suckle followed by swallowing allows the child to suck on a nipple and then use the muscles in her tongue and throat to swallow the liquid. When something like a finger or a nipple comes into contact with the back of an infant's tongue she will gag reflexively. This gag reflex keeps the infant from choking and is easily activated in very young infants.

The suckle and swallow are the most common sources of feeding difficulty in infants with developmental delays. For an infant who is unable to close her lips or swallow liquid when it is presented, feeding becomes very problematic. **Tongue thrust**, which is the forceful protrusion of the tongue, may also interfere with the infant's ability to swallow correctly. In addition, other problems that may interfere with suckle and swallow include respiratory or breathing difficulties or a lack of ability to coordinate the mouth and lips. A speech pathologist or occupational therapist can help when the infant has a significant problem that interferes with her ability to suck from a bottle and swallow appropriately. They may recommend a specialized nipple or they may suggest positioning a child in such a way that it makes it easier for her to take liquid into her mouth.

As the infant matures, her suckle response becomes much more coordinated and almost rhythmic in nature. In addition, she learns to consume liquid much more rapidly. By the time she is two to three months old, she should be able to swallow about 8 ounces of liquid in 20–30 minutes. Infants with developmental delays or immature patterns of suckle and swallow will be less coordinated; their sucking and swallowing will not be rhythmic. In addition, they may swallow less than 8 ounces at a time and take much longer to feed.

Birth to 6 Months

For the first 4 to 6 months, it is best to hold an infant when she is feeding. This is a special time when you can bond with the child by talking softly or singing to her and making eye contact while holding her securely in your arms. In some cases, if the infant has severe difficulties with breathing, sucking, or swallowing, the speech pathologist may recommend that an infant be positioned in a more upright position that enables her to take in liquid more easily. Other children with special needs may have a temperament that makes them resistant to being held or touched. For children who exhibit tactile sensitivity, feeding them while they are in a baby carrier or wrapping them snugly in a blanket during feeding may be recommended. While social interaction is crucial, the primary objective for a child with special needs is that she receives the nutrition necessary to grow and develop. Without proper nutrients, the infant may not gain weight and the development of muscles and tissues may be at risk.

Between four and six months, the infant begins to anticipate eating. She may open her mouth when she sees a bottle or spoon, and in some cases move her body toward the food. The introduction of food other than a bottle may take place during this time, but varies depending on the child's development. Children with very sensitive digestive systems or with very immature motor development may remain on a bottle for a much longer time without being introduced to solid food. For infants who continue to have difficulty coordinating their lips, jaw, and tongue muscles, choking or gagging can become a major obstacle during feeding time. Choking is discussed more fully on page 75 in this chapter.

7 to 9 Months

By 7 months of age, most children are eating some baby food from a spoon. Initially, this may be cereal mixed with formula or soft foods, such as applesauce or pureed fruit. Children with very sensitive digestive systems or with severe allergies may be placed on a special diet. Sometime between seven and nine months, a typically developing child may start to eat finger foods. As finger foods and more solid foods are introduced into the diet, infants begin to move food from one side of the mouth to the other before they chew and swallow it. In addition, most infants begin to show a preference for certain foods. They will show this preference by moving their body toward a preferred food when it is presented or by spitting out a food they do not like. Adults may notice an attempt by the child to munch food on the gums. As the infant gains upper lip control she will begin to try to drink from a cup and may even reach up and try to help an adult hold the cup. Children who are not ready for drinking from a cup may still try to help feed themselves by attempting to hold their own bottle.

10 to 15 Months

Between 10 and 12 months, the infant develops a controlled biting pattern. However, this biting really only applies to softer foods. By the time an infant is about 15 months old, she should be able to feed herself using her fingers, bite through most soft foods, drink from a cup, and exhibit a **rotary chewing pattern** when eating. Self-feeding is rudimentary and exploratory; therefore, it will be messy. The ability to bite and chew harder more solid foods does not occur until closer to two years of age. Children with developmental delays may have two problems in relation to biting food: 1) a **tonic bite reflex**, and 2) a **phasic bite reflex** or false bite.

A tonic bite reflex occurs when there is a sudden tense bite and the infant appears unable to release the bite and open her jaws naturally. As the teeth and gums are touched, the child tenses and clenches her mouth shut even more. This response is often characteristic of an infant who has issues related to tactile defensiveness. **Note:** *When feeding a child with a tonic bite reflex, never attempt to release the bite by putting your fingers in the child's mouth. Nor should you attempt to pull a spoon from the child's mouth if she has bitten down on it.* Such actions actually provide more stimulation and make the situation worse. Instead, wait to see if the infant will release the bite reflex voluntarily. If, after a few seconds, this does not occur, apply light pressure to the muscles at the back of the jaw. This can be done by placing your fingertips on the child's face near the jaw muscles. In addition, tilting the child's head forward may also enable her to relax her bite.

A phasic bite is a reflex that is often seen in much younger infants and is the result of pressure on the gums. This pressure causes a rhythmic opening and closing of the jaws. This reflex should be gone by the time the child is about six months old and is not considered a functional or useful bite; it is, instead, a response to stimulation. In other words the opening and closing of the jaws is not intentional and is caused by the stimulation to the gums. Often, children with developmental delays will have a phasic bite reflex for a much longer time, resulting in difficulty introducing solid foods.

15 to 24 Months

Between 15 and 24 months of age, the tongue and jaw movements become increasingly more coordinated and, as a result, self-feeding becomes more refined. Because the child can close her lips around the rim of a cup, she is likely to spill less, and she may begin to experiment with eating foods of various textures. Chewing is also more consistent and eating solid foods becomes easier. It is recommended that lumpy and chopped foods be introduced prior to introducing more solid foods that require chewing. This is especially true for infants with immature motor skills, as they will need time and practice before they are able to chew solid foods.

Issues Associated with Eating

Choking is always a concern when feeding a child. This is certainly true if the child has special needs. If unattended, choking can lead to a loss of oxygen to the brain and death. Should a child begin to choke, do not pat her on the back, as this may cause the object to become lodged in her throat. Under no circumstances should you attempt to turn the child upside down, as this too may result in serious consequences. It is critical, in all early childhood settings, especially those serving young children with special needs, that caregivers are trained in specific methods for dealing with choking. Unless you have proper training, do not attempt to perform the **Heimlich maneuver** on anyone. Using the Heimlich without training could result in damage to internal organs and in some cases death. The main objective, should choking occur, is to stay calm and make sure the child is getting air. Table 6–1 on the following pages shows feeding and eating issues that children with special needs may experience.

Make meal time a social time.

Table 6–1 *Feeding and Eating Issues for Children with Special Needs*

Special Need	Feeding and Eating Issues	Suggestions
Low birth weight/ premature infants	• Central nervous system immaturity may lead to the infant's inability to suck, swallow, or chew. • Rooting reflex may be weak, resulting in the infant taking longer to feed. • Insufficient sucking patterns often result in poor weight gain.	• Intake of food may be diminished because of poor motor skills, resulting in a need to feed more frequently. • Allow extra time for feeding.
Cleft lip and/or cleft palate	• Depending on the location and degree of the cleft, the infant may not be able to coordinate motor movements. • Sucking may be diminished. • Because of the cleft in the palate, food may collect on the roof of the mouth and be expelled through the nose, resulting in choking, spitting, or vomiting.	• Most likely, the infant will require a specialized nipple for bottle feeding. • Initially, feeding may require assistance from a speech-language pathologist or occupational therapist.
Cerebral palsy	• Depending on the type of muscle damage, the infant may not be able to swallow, root, suckle, or chew properly. • Hypersensitivity to touch may lessen the infant's ability to take in food, resulting in poor weight gain. • If the child has poor voluntary muscle control, self-feeding and chewing may also be affected.	• A physical therapist or speech pathologist can help you learn to feed a child with cerebral palsy. • It is important that the child is placed to facilitate symmetry and midline positioning. Try sitting in front of a table with your feet resting on a stool. Place the infant facing you on your lap with her body semi-reclined on a pillow propped against your legs or the table. • Have the child sit with her legs bent (flexed). Present food to her from her midline, not off to one side. • For older children, it may be necessary to use a specialized chair and facilitate movement of the jaw muscles with your fingers placed on the child's chin and jaw.

Table 6-1 *Feeding and Eating Issues for Children with Special Needs (continued)*

Special Need	Feeding and Eating Issues	Suggestions
Down syndrome	• Thickened tongue may result in difficulty sucking, chewing, or swallowing. • Some children try to eat too fast and consume too much food, which results in upset stomach or choking. • Low muscle tone may cause the mouth to hang open, which results in difficulty with drinking from a cup and swallowing. • Overall, the muscles of the jaw, tongue, and throat may not be coordinated well, resulting in poor eating and gagging.	• Prepare the child for mealtime by using a consistent routine. • Pace the feeding and learn to recognize when the child is full. • A child with Down syndrome will need extra help learning to feed herself and in practicing chewing small bites with her mouth closed. • The child may require extra encouragement to try such things as holding a cup independently, trying new foods, and learning to stop eating when she is full.
Autism spectrum disorder	• May be picky eaters or only want foods of a specific texture. • May not be interested in food in the typical way.	• Provide opportunities to encounter new foods and allow her to experiment with food. • Allow extra time for eating and have an organized plan if the child reacts to being fed by having a tantrum or throwing food on the floor.
Sensory impairments (vision)	• Being unable to see a bottle or nipple may interfere with eating. • Because the child may not respond by looking at you when you are feeding her, typical bonding may take more time.	• Be consistent when setting the table and presenting foods; this fosters independence. • Use child-sized utensils and good lighting to help maximize residual vision. • Place dishes on a placemat and help the child feel the edges, so she can learn the boundaries for her dishes. Also, try dishes with suction cups that anchor them to the table. • Initially, as new foods are presented, allow the child to touch, smell, and experiment with the new food, as this helps the child learn more about that food and its texture. • When she gets older, teach the child how to pour by using a small pitcher and showing her how to place one finger inside her cup to feel when the liquid is near the top.

Feeding Tubes

Sometimes, a child may be fed through a tube because of anatomical problems that prevent feeding by mouth. These problems may include:

- Underdeveloped respiratory system,
- **Gastroesophageal reflux disease (GERD)**,
- Severe cleft palate and/or cleft lip,
- Cardiac defects,
- Severe muscle issues, such as not being able to voluntarily control the muscles of the tongue, jaw or lips, or
- General **failure to thrive** or faltering growth, a medical term used to describe an infant who is a not gaining weight and whose physical growth failure over an extended period of time is much slower than expected.

A feeding tube is a medical device used to provide nutrition to infants who cannot or do not obtain nutrition orally. The state of being fed by a feeding tube is called **enteral feeding** or tube feeding. In such cases, the tube, referred to as a gastrointestinal tube, may be inserted in a variety of ways. The three most common include the **nasogastric tube (NG Tube)**, which is inserted through the nostril and passes to the stomach; an **oral gastric tube**, which passes from the mouth directly to the stomach; or a **gastrostomy tube (GT Tube)**, which is placed through the abdominal wall directly into the stomach. Tube-fed infants often develop other issues as a result of being fed through a tube. For example, they will not have the same opportunities to develop their lip, throat, and tongue muscles that other children experience. They will also have considerable difficulty adjusting to foods of varying tastes and textures once the tube is removed. Tube-fed infants are also at-risk for a number of complications as a result of the tube feeding. For example, if they are fed too rapidly they may develop severe diarrhea. Bacterial infections may result from tubes that are not cleaned properly, and constipation can indicate that too little fluid is consumed.

If a child with a tube is in your care, it is important to understand the following:

- The infant may try to pull out the tube. Taping the tube to the child's face all the way from the edge of the nose to the ear can make the nasogastric tube more secure.
- Tape can irritate the skin. There are many types of tape available. The child's family will likely have already found one that works well by the time she comes into your classroom. *Uni-Solve* adhesive remover pads are often used to help take off old tape more gently.
- Tubes can get in the way of everyday activities. Looping up the extra tubing, securing it with the end cap, and using a safety pin to attach it to the child's clothing on her shoulder can help alleviate this.
- Tubes can cause greater oral and facial aversions for a child who may be orally defensive in the first place.
- Sucking on a pacifier can be comforting for a child with a tube, especially during feeding.

Teaching Infants, Toddlers, and Twos with Special Needs

- Remember, in most cases, tubes are temporary and the ultimate goal is to remove the tube so the child can learn to eat on her own.

Because infants who are tube-fed do not have the same opportunities to bond that others infants experience during more traditional feeding time, it is critical to talk to them, sing to them, and cuddle them, both before and after they are fed. In addition, learn any special instructions about how to tube feed and what signs to look for that indicate the infant is in distress or discomfort. Again, a nutritionist or occupational therapist is a good resource for information about tube feeding. The occupational therapist can also guide you in planning additional oral motor exercises that help the child replace those usually performed during feeding and eating.

Self-Feeding

As toddlers become more independent, they begin to show an increased interest in self-feeding. A toddler with cognitive, motor, emotional, or sensory issues may not acquire self-feeding skills as easily as her peers. There may even be a tendency to discourage self-feeding because it takes too long for the child to eat or because it is easier to feed the child. However, it is very important to recognize that learning to feed herself is one of the most important skills a young child with special needs can learn; it is a skill she will use throughout her life. Because a child may be developmentally delayed, it is often difficult to decide exactly when to stop feeding the child and begin to encourage her to learn to feed herself. A team meeting can help determine when it is time to start this

Self-feeding is a critical functional skills for young children with special needs.

process. The team may consist of you, the child's family, and appropriate therapists, such as occupational therapy, speech therapy, physical therapy, or home-health nursing. Many factors determine when to begin the process. For example, some children are not psychologically or emotionally ready to learn to self-feed, even if they have the motor skills. Several indicators can help the team make a decision: the child's hand-to-mouth behavior, her ability to bring objects to her mouth and to grasp, her interest in self-feeding, her overall oral-motor development, and how well she tolerates meal time. According to Bailey and Wolery (1992), it is important to follow these guidelines when teaching self-feeding:

- Teach spoon and cup use first, as these are the easiest skills to acquire.
- Recognize that self-feeding is not a discrete task in itself; it is made up of a series of events in which each task builds on the one before it.
- Use physical prompts to help a child learn a sequence. For example, rather than dipping a spoon in applesauce and handing it to the child to feed herself, hold the child's hand around the spoon and let her dip it into the applesauce with you. Then, keep your hand on the spoon and help guide it to her mouth. Eventually, you can fade out your prompts and encourage the child to do more of the whole task alone.
- Initially, use foods that are reinforcing to the child. In other words, teach her to eat her preferred foods before going on to the lesser preferred ones.
- Remember to teach the child how to pace her eating, as this is important both socially and nutritionally.

Adaptations

Certain physical conditions may require that the child eat using adaptive utensils, such as a special spoon, a cup with two handles, or a plate that makes it easier to scoop food from the inside. Cups that are appropriate include those that do not require the child to tilt her head back to drink from them. Tilting the head may result in spilling; it may also lead to the child's choking on the liquid. For children who need an adapted cup, one is easily made by cutting a "U" shape on one side of the cup. These cups should be constructed of thick plastic. Raising or curving the side of a plate may make it easier for a child to scoop out food. Spoons can be bought or made with various handles to accommodate children with motor and grasp issues. One simple adaptation is to remove the inside clip of a foam hair roller and place the roller around a spoon. This produces a larger handle for the child to use.

It is important to remember that proper positioning is critical for helping a child eat independently. She should be seated so that her spine is in alignment and she has optimal use of her hands and arms. Her feet should be secure and she should have her trunk supported so that she is able to reach her eating utensils. A child with poor head control may require additional support so her head is positioned upright. Under no circumstances should a child eat or be fed with her head leaning backward. While this is not dangerous, it is not conducive to proper digestion.

Making Eating a Social Time

Mealtime and snack time are not only opportunities to teach proper eating skills, they are also times when infants, toddlers, and two-year-olds learn valuable social interaction skills. To make mealtime enjoyable and rewarding, try to involve the child in helping with preparation. Encourage her to play an active role by helping distribute placemats, napkins, cups, or utensils. This is also a time for you to help the child learn new words and communicate. Talk about what you are doing, encourage the child with special needs to watch you as you do something, then ask her to model what you just did. If at all possible, allow children to serve themselves and make basic choices about what they want to eat. Remember, this is an excellent time to teach requesting skills and reinforce the use of "please" and "thank you."

Summary

Some general guidelines for feeding infants, toddlers, and two-year-olds with special needs include:

- For toddlers and two-year-olds who may be resistant to new foods, look for opportunities to learn about new foods, such as playing a smelling game. Encourage tasting games where each child takes a small bite of a new or unfamiliar food.
- Make mealtime a nurturing, playful, and positive time together. Avoid getting overly concerned if the child does not eat enough. Accept the fact that you may have to allow extra time for the child with special needs to eat.
- Offer choices whenever possible. Choice-making is a critical skill and reinforces independence. Practice offering the child two different foods on two spoons, let her smell the food, and then honor her choice. Remember, she may not choose the preferred food by vocalization; instead, she might lean her body toward the food.
- Use mealtime as an opportunity to communicate. Be positive and talk about what the child is eating. Do not coerce the child to eat, and avoid commenting on how much or how little she eats.
- Realize that some young children are **neophobic** (psychologically afraid of new activities) about food and may require extra opportunities before they feel secure enough to try a new food.
- Offer opportunities for infants, toddlers, and two-year-olds to practice eating independently and do not be concerned about the "mess." Remember that the main idea is to eat the food. There will be time, later, to deal with how they eat it.

Terms Used in This Chapter

autism spectrum disorder— refers to the whole range of symptoms which are characteristics of autism. These characteristics will differ and can range from very mild to quite severe.

cerebral palsy—Used to describe a group of conditions affecting body movements and muscle coordination. It is caused by damage to one or more specific areas of the brain, usually occurring before, during, or shortly after birth.

cleft lip or **cleft palate**—An opening in the roof of the mouth (the palate), due to a failure of the palatal to close from either side of the mouth. The opening may extend through the lips, resulting in a cleft lip as well.

Down syndrome—A chromosome disorder caused by an extra chromosome number 21, which affects both the physical and intellectual development of the child. Characteristics include mental retardation, a characteristic face, and multiple malformations.

enteral feeding—Another term for tube feeding or gastrointestinal tube feeding in which a tube is inserted into the child's stomach so that she can receive nutrition.

failure to thrive—A medical term used to describe poor weight gain and physical growth failure over a long period of time in infancy. The term faltering growth is often used to describe the same condition.

gag reflex (faucial reflex)—An automatic response to anything that comes into contact with the muscles at the back of the tongue or throat. This reflex is very sensitive in infants.

gastroesophageal reflux disease (GERD)—Chronic symptoms or mucosal damage produced by abnormal reflux of gastric contents into the esophagus.

gastrointestinal tube—A long plastic tube that may be inserted into the infant's digestive tract through which nutrition may be given, usually with a syringe.

gastrostomy tube (GT Tube)—A type of gastrointestinal tube that is placed through the abdominal wall directly into the digestive tract or stomach.

Heimlich maneuver—An emergency technique for preventing suffocation when a person's airway (windpipe) becomes blocked by a piece of food or other object. It can usually be used safely on children over the age of one. The Heimlich is never to be used without proper training, as it could result in damage to internal organs and, in some cases, death.

nasogastric tube (NG Tube)—A type of tube inserted through the nostril and passed into the stomach so the child can receive nutrition.

neophobic—An intense aversion or phobia, which is unfounded and unexplainable, to a new activity or item.

nutritionist—A person who plans for special meals or helps parents identify appropriate foods for children with special dietary needs.

occupational therapist—A health professional who is trained to help people do the day-to-day tasks that "occupy" their time such as eating or dressing yourself.

oral gastric tube—A type of gastrointestinal tube that passes from the mouth directly to the stomach.

Teaching Infants, Toddlers, and Twos with Special Needs

phasic bite reflex—Pressure on the gums that causes a rhythmic opening and closing of the jaws.

physical therapist—A health professional who uses specially designed exercises and equipment to help patients regain or improve their physical abilities.

rooting reflex—An early infantile reflex that causes the child to turn her head toward the source of food.

rotary chewing pattern—A normal development pattern in learning to chew whereby diagonal movement of the jaw occurs as food is moved to the side or center of the mouth.

sensory impairments—A disability that affects a specific sense such as vision or hearing.

speech-language pathologist—A specialist who works with a child with speech and/or language delays.

tongue thrust—The forceful protrusion of the tongue through the lips. This response can interfere with bottle feeding and swallowing.

tonic bite reflex—Occurs when there is a sudden tense bite and the infant appears unable to release the bite and open her jaws naturally.

Resources Used in This Chapter

Bailey, D. B., & Wolery, M. (1992). *Teaching infants and preschoolers with disabilities (2nd Edition)*. Upper Saddle River, NJ: Merrill-Prentice Hall.

Ernsperger, L., & Stegen-Hanson, T. (2004). *Just take a bite: Easy, effective answers to food aversions and eating challenges*. Arlington, TX: Future Horizons.

Pogrund, R. L., & Fazzi, D. L. (2002). *Early focus: Working with young children who are blind or visually impaired children and their families*. New York: AFB Press.

For More Information

Klein, M. D. (2007). Tube feeding transition plateaus. *Exceptional Parent, 37*(2), 22–25.

Waldman, H. B., & Perlman, S. P. (2007). Baby fat may be cute, but chubby kids could be in jeopardy, and for children with disabilities. *Exceptional Parent, 37*(2), 12–14.

Wallace, L. S. (2007). FAT: The good, the bad and the trans fat truth and how it applies to people with special needs. *Exceptional Parent, 37*(2), 15, 19–20.

Teaching Infants, Toddlers, and Twos with Special Needs

Communication

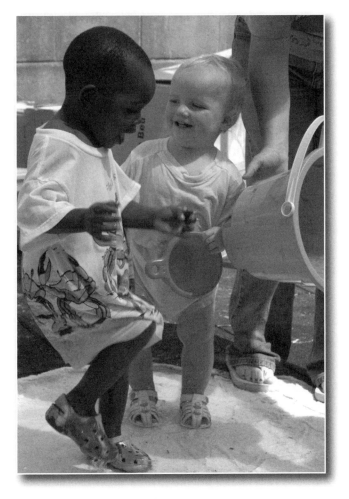

Expressing pleasure is a way to communicate with peers.

An Overview of Communication

Even before they arrive, infants begin to communicate. For example, when an expectant mother rubs her tummy, the infant may communicate with a kick. This response, though primitive, is a form of communication. In fact, by using the **fetal heart rate test** to track an unborn baby's heart rate, researchers have discovered that, upon hearing the sound of the mother's voice, an unborn child's heart rate will decrease, indicating a calming effect (Fitzpatrick, 2002). For that reason, introducing the unborn baby to different sounds may well play a role in his future speech and language development. Reading stories, singing songs, and talking to the baby promote his developing communication skills, even before birth.

— Note —

The first time a term is used in this chapter it appears in bold. All terms in bold are defined at the end of this chapter, beginning on page 96.

At birth, an infant begins to vocalize. Most of his initial vocalizations are in the form of crying, which is his way to indicate discomfort. However, at this stage the child has not yet associated the adult's attending to his needs as being a direct result of his crying. As he matures, however, the infant learns that when he cries, someone appears to take care of him. These responses to his cries not only help the child learn to communicate (non-verbal), but also help him understand that communication is reciprocal—that it involves a communicator (in this case the infant) and a receiver (the adult). While he does not understand the terminology, he has certainly learned how to solicit a response by communicating an action.

From birth until about 4 months of age, this communication continues to consist mainly of **reflexive crying**, or crying without intent, in an effort to express feelings (Fitzpatrick, 2002). However, it is important to continue speaking and singing to the baby, as these activities give him even more exposure to the sounds of language. Activities such as reproducing the baby's sounds (repeating back what you hear from him), responding to his communication in its various forms, and answering his cries are all ways to start an infant on the road to **intentional communication,** in which the infant deliberately attempts to communicate a want or need using either words, gestures or other methods of communication.

Soon, the infant will start experimenting with sounds and demonstrate his newly emerging skill by "babbling." Much of how he continues to practice his newly forming language skills depends on the way you react and respond to his communication attempts. It is very important to respond to infants in a way that is child centered. You should follow the infant's lead, so that when he babbles, you imitate this sound by making the same babbling sound. Other ways to engage infants in a child-centered context include:

- Involving infants in daily routines, which should include greetings and saying "Bye-bye" when you leave the room.
- Asking questions, waiting, and then answering the question for the infant. For example, ask, "Ohhh, you need a diaper change, don't you?" Wait a few seconds, reach down, pick up the infant, and then say, "Yes you do. You'll feel better when you are all clean and dry!"
- Adjusting your tone of speech by using "baby talk" and singing silly songs.
- Trying to interpret unintelligible utterances. For example, if the infant says, "ma-moo-ma-moo" and ask, "You want your bottle, don't you?"

Older infants learn to communicate in a "situation-centered context." In this form, you do not repeat the infant's vocal patterns and babbling, but speak to him using regular adult language. This allows you to be sensitive to the infant's needs while you model the correct way language is used.

By 14 to 20 months of age, a child will usually speak actual words. He begins with simple words he has heard often, such as "mama" or "dada." It is not unusual for them to approximate words, such as saying "baba" for "bottle." As they learn more words, they will eventually combine them into two-word phrases, such as "come baby" or "doggie gone." These types of phrases usually begin around age two. From there, language skills seem to grow and become more sophisticated on an almost daily basis. At this point, an infant should have around 50 words in his vocabulary, while some infants may know as many as 200 words. Infants with special needs generally tend to develop vocabulary more slowly than their peers, and often require more practice to add new words to their vocabulary.

Once a toddler can link two words together, things begin to develop very rapidly. First, as the child discovers that everything has a name, he begins to show an understanding of both words and content. Next, the toddler learns that object words and action words can be combined to have different meanings. It is important to note that children may not progress through these beginning stages of communication in a traditional manner. Some children will experience marked delays in how and when they acquire language; the primary form of communication, for others, may be spoken speech. For that reason, it is important to understand exactly how an inability to communicate may impact a child with special needs.

What Is Communication?

Communication is an interaction between two or more people, where information is sent between one person and another. The most common method of conveying information is through speech with the use of verbal language. Delayed speech and/or language development is very common in young children with special needs. Therefore, it is important to recognize that communication may indeed be primarily non-verbal for many children with special needs. How well any child communicates depends on three essential elements of communication—form, function, and content. Knowing these elements will make it easier to understand not only how, but why, a very young child communicates. Table 7–1 illustrates the elements.

Pointing can be an early form of communication.

Table 7-1 *Elements of Communication*

Element	Definition	Example
Form	A way to communicate	Crying, talking, gesturing, sign language, and pointing to picture cards
Function	A reason to communicate	Is hungry, wants something, needs something or someone, and needs attention
Content	Something to communicate about	Experiences and opportunities to explore, which provide the child with something to communicate about

Understanding the Child's "Form" of Communication

For some children with special needs, the form of communication they use will be speech. However, unlike their typically developing peers, it may be delayed (such as when a child does not learn to use many functional or useable words). In some cases, the child's speech may be unintelligible (such as when the child's speech is so incomprehensible that

Peer interactions can occur in many ways.

it cannot be readily understood by others). Speech and articulation have different meanings and should not be confused. Generally, speech is the sound generated when we talk. **Articulation** has to do with how sounds are pronounced. When the sounds within words cannot be understood, it is referred to as **misarticulation**. In fact, the most common speech delay found in older preschool-age children is an articulation delay, such as when a child says "wookie" instead of "cookie."

However, as many young children learn to talk, misarticulating is a normal part of the process. For that reason, knowing which sounds are "typical" for a child's age and stage of development is important. There have been a number of diverse studies that have attempted to identify when a particular sound should be mastered by most children. Because all children develop at their own same pace, there is a range in which specific sounds are thought to emerge. Prather, Hendrick, and Kern (1975) divided speech sounds into three categories: early eight; middle eight, and late eight. According to their research, the early eight sounds include the sounds that the letters m, b, j, w, n, d, p, and h make. Most children master these sounds by age three. The middle eight and late eight sounds usually are not mastered until after age three, and will not be discussed here.

The term **intelligibility** refers to the proportion of a child's speech that a listener can readily understand. As toddlers continue to learn and use words to communicate, the ability of those around them to understand what they are saying steadily increases. However, in young children, there are factors that can often influence a child's intelligibility:

- Whether speech is single word or conversational speech;
- When speaking to family members or care providers is much different than when the child speaks to unfamiliar listeners;
- Whether the child is speaking about familiar or unfamiliar conversational topics; and
- Whether or not a topic is of interest to the child.

A few "red flags" can indicate that a child of 36 months may have an articulation problem that is beyond the scope of typical development, including:

- Not talking clearly enough for you or other adults to understand anything that is said,
- Not talking or attempting to make sounds at all,
- An inability to combine common sounds into words, and
- An inability to produce enough speech sounds to combine them into words.

Most important, if a child is not attempting to speak by the time he is 24–36 months, he may need to learn an alternative means of communication. This could include sign language or using pictures to let others know what he wants and needs. Learning an alternative way to communicate will not, in any way, keep a child from eventually developing speech. In fact, the alternative form of communication may be just the bridge he needs to help the child learn to talk. Being unable to communicate may interfere with the development of a child with special needs and can result in frustration and behaviors (such as tantrums), which would not otherwise occur.

Function and Content of Communication

The reason a child communicates and what he communicates about depends on how he uses words, pictures, or signs to convey his message. Communication generally has two components: **receptive language** and **expressive language**. Receptive language is how well a child understands what is being said by someone talking to him. Expressive language has to do with how well a child uses or responds with words and sentences. Research has shown that children develop receptive language long before they develop expressive language. For this reason, it is critical to talk to a child from the moment of his birth.

The term **language delay** is generally used to describe a child whose language is not developing in the right sequence, or developing at a slower rate than his peers. A **language disorder** describes atypical language development, such as using limited language, not using words at all, or not combining words into sentences. To accurately determine if a child has a language delay, a speech pathologist may take a **language sample**. This involves recording a series of utterances (usually 200 or more), and analyzing the mean length of utterance (average length of a sentence) as well as the types of words used (nouns, verbs, pronouns, adjectives). Because it is taken in context and not in an artificial environment, it is believed to be a more accurate method to identify language development than simply showing a child a picture and asking him to describe it. There are generally four components that are considered part of language acquisition. Both receptive and expressive language use these four basic structural components:

1. *Phonology*: The system of sound segments that humans use to accumulate words. Each language has a different set of these segments, or phonemes. Infants quickly learn to recognize and then produce the speech segments that are characteristic of their native language. In fact, brain research indicates that by the time a child is nine months old, he recognizes sounds characteristic to his native language (Schiller, 1999).

2. *Semantics*: The system of meanings that are expressed by words and phrases. Words must have a shared or conventional meaning to be useful for conversation. Conventional meaning may be specific to the sub-culture or geographic location in which a child lives. For example, the word "pop" may mean soda pop in some areas, while the same word "pop" may mean father in other areas. That is why language is best learned in context, rather than in isolation. Picking out the correct meaning for each new word is a major learning task for many toddlers. Research has shown a direct correlation between the number of words a child hears by a given age and his later language acquisition (Singer, Golinkoff, & Hirsh-Pasek, 2006).

3. *Grammar*: The system of rules by which words and phrases are arranged to make meaningful statements. Generally speaking, toddlers will learn the names of things (nouns) first, and then begin to assign action words (verbs) to their actions. Adjectives and descriptive words develop later as the child experiments and uses language as a means to get what he needs or wants and as a means to describe his world and the people in it.

4. *Pragmatics*: The system of patterns that determine how humans use language in particular social settings for particular conversational purposes. Children learn that conversations customarily begin with a greeting and require reciprocity. In addition, they learn that conversation usually involves a shared topic. With practice, children learn to adjust the content of their communication to match their listener's interests, knowledge, and language ability. Pragmatics is considered by many to be the most difficult aspect of language for a child with special needs to master because what is appropriate for one social context may not be appropriate for others.

How This Relates to Young Children with Special Needs

For infants with special needs, especially those with sensory impairments or severe motor delays, it may be difficult to know how to respond to their needs. That is why the most important thing you can do is to know as much as possible about the child before he comes to the classroom. By knowing how to interpret his movements, sounds, cries, and gestures, it will be much easier to know what he needs and respond to those needs.

An infant with cognitive delays needs a caregiver who knows how to interpret the unique manner in which that child communicates. This could include such things as recognizing that when the child moves his body a certain way he is requesting more food, or when he screams at a certain pitch, he is indicating that he is "finished."

As infants begin to transition from unintentional communication to a more deliberate attempt to engage others, it is vital that adults continue to respond consistently to the child's cries, smiles, and movements as if they were intentional. In time, those unintentional attempts to communicate will become more deliberate and planned. Some of the key elements that infants, toddlers, and two-year-olds need to learn to communicate effectively include:

- An understanding or reciprocity of turn-taking sequences with adults;
- Anticipation about how adults will respond to a given behavior, so that, when an infant repeats it, he will get a desired response;
- Mutual engagement with toys such as when a child and adult play with a toy together; and
- A concrete understanding that the response by an adult is a direct result of an action by the infant.

An infant with special needs may initially use a gesture or random babbling to communicate an intention or need. However, as he matures and experiments with sounds, he will begin to make speech sounds that approximate words. Appropriate goals for 12- to 18-month-olds with developmental delays include:

- Making a conscious attempt to control the behavior of others, usually adults, by requesting something, protesting, or rejecting an activity outright.
- Using social communication, characterized by the child's attempt to keep an adult's attention focused on him by talking, laughing, or making a gesture of some kind.
- Attempting joint attention or shared communication, including directing an adult's attention toward something that is of interest to the child.
- Use of gestures to communicate, such as reaching his hands out to indicate "I want."

As a child with special needs learns more about cause and effect, he begins to understand that what he says or does can influence other people and his environment. During this stage, a child starts to see communication as a means to get what he wants. Goals for a child at this stage may include:

- Introducing and using **picture sequence cards** as a way to communicate
- Learning basic sign language as a method of communication.
- Understanding that "nothing is free" and that he must ask for what he wants. His way of asking may be to grab your hand and pull you toward what he wants. Nonetheless, he is still required to perform some kind of action to indicate his need.
- Attempting to say a few basic words.
- Using his body to communicate, such as leaning toward the spoon as you feed him in an effort to indicate "I want more."
- Beginning to sign the word "more" with actions, such as putting his hands together.

While most children with special needs will not move much beyond these stages during their toddler years, it is possible that some may develop more sophisticated ways to communicate. In order to do so, they must first understand that repeating a particular action, gesture, or word usually gets the same result. It is also important that the child begin to attempt to imitate language as he hears it. He may attempt to put two words together and show some elation in repeating what he has just heard. These interactions should be encouraged, and certainly warrant praise from you. Once a child understands these concepts, he can learn to communicate by:

- Taking turns;
- Understanding the names of those familiar to him;
- Repeating what he just heard;
- Using gestures more consistently, such as shaking his head to indicate "no";
- Answering simple questions;

- Asking for something or requesting that you continue something; and
- Using words or signs in a more meaningful way.

With practice and patience, children with special needs may eventually learn to communicate in some of these ways, although they may be older preschoolers before they:

- Intentionally use words to greet others, ask for something, or protest something;
- Ask questions, or tell you about something;
- Express ideas and feelings that are relevant to them;
- Have short conversations (although children with autism will always be more easily distracted than their peers);
- Repeat something if he thinks the listener does not understand; and
- Start to use longer sentences with more descriptive words.

Augmentative Communication

What About Children Who Are Non-Verbal?

Some children with special needs will never use spoken language as their primary form of communication. For these children, it may be necessary to use alternative or **augmentative forms of communication**, which are generally categorized as **low-tech** or **high-tech**. Low-tech methods of communication include pictures or objects, which the child either points to as a way to tell you what he wants or needs. High-tech communication methods generally involve a battery-operated device that the child activates in some manner, as in a computer that talks for him.

Low-Tech Methods of Communication

While sign language is certainly one method that can be functional for the child who is non-verbal, pictures are clearly more universal. Anyone, including a child's peer, can understand that if a child with special needs points to a picture of a toy, it means he would like to play with the toy. Handing a picture to a communication partner is another way the child can interact with that partner. Pictures are used in various ways:

- To make communication boards;
- For schedules, including embedded schedules;
- In combinations, in an effort to describe concepts and ideas;
- To indicate a choice or a preference; and
- As an answer to a question.

Pictures are not only practical and simple to use, they also provide a sense of consistency, because the same set of pictures used at school can also be used at home. When using a **picture communication system**, you will want to refer to the guidelines in Table 7–2.

Table 7-2 *Guidelines for Using a Picture Communication System*

General uses for pictures	• To help the child learn daily routines • To sequence an activity • To introduce a new word • To provide an added clue for children with special needs
Pictures as a way to initiate a conversation with someone	• Once the child becomes more familiar with the pictures in the classroom, try to encourage him to use them to start a communication interaction. • Model using pictures with small groups of children.
Consistently use the same pictures with each individual child	• Consistency and practice will reinforce the child's use of the picture cards. • Send picture cards home and encourage the child's family to use them as well.
Continually build opportunities for the child to use and expand his vocabulary and skills through pictures	• Ask questions that require the child to answer by pointing to a picture card. • Expand the child's repertoire of pictures by including action pictures and pictures that can be used to tell you what and how the child is feeling.

How Do I Help a Child with Special Needs Use Pictures to Communicate?

The most widely-recognized formal system of communication is the Picture Exchange System (PECS), developed by Andy Bondy and Lori Frost. In the PECS system, a child presents pictures to a partner or selects pictures from a board or portable notebook. The pictures are inexpensive and portable, allowing the child to use them in a variety of different situations. While pictures are an excellent teaching tool for children with special needs, the PECS system offers more options. Because there is a specific method involved in presenting each sequence of pictures using the official PECS system, special training is required.

An alternative to the PECS system may be a simple **communication board** that uses laminated pictures taken with a camera. A communication board is a tool that can easily be used by a child who does not have verbal communication skills (Gould & Sullivan, 1999). Begin by using one or two pictures and work up to using more, and then experiment to determine if the child responds best to real pictures or black-and-white line drawings. This is important because some children with special needs have difficulty understanding that a drawing is a representation of a real object. In some cases, a child may not respond to either pictures or drawings and it will be necessary to use real objects instead of pictures.

High-Tech Methods of Communication

Traditionally, young children with special needs do not use high-tech electronic communication devices. There are, however, a few products that can be used appropriately with young children, including devices with the capacity to deliver a single message or, in some cases, devices that can be programmed to deliver several messages.

Single-message switches, such as the "Big-Mack Jellybean Switch" by Ablenet, are sometimes used to help children as they begin to communicate. It is a button-type switch controlling a recorder on which a single message has been recorded. The child is taught to push the button, with the result being that the message is "spoken." Unlike more expensive devices, this switch can be used with multiple children, and it is often used when they are learning to indicate the need to go to the bathroom. A picture of a bathroom or toilet can be easily attached to the switch. Whenever any child needs to go, they just walk up to the switch and push the button. The message is simple to change and the device is easy to operate. Multiple-message devices include the "Speak-Easy" and the "Talking Photo Album." These easy-to-use electronic devices allow more than one message to be recorded, and the messages can be changed whenever necessary. Regardless of which device is used, it is important to start by teaching the child to use only one or two messages, adding more as the child learns to use the device more independently.

Summary

It is often difficult to know which goals to set when a child is learning to communicate. If you know which concepts are critical for communication development, the job will be easier. While each child is unique and will communicate in his own way, there are several general suggestions to think about when setting communication goals for infants, toddlers, and two-year-olds with special needs:

- Communication is most effective when it involves interaction with others who are able to understand the communication methods used (language, signs, movements, pictures, objects, and so on). Learning to interact with other people is a life skill that the child can build on and use throughout his life. You play an important role in helping the child learn these skills.
- To communicate effectively, the child must have a reliable form or way to communicate (see above discussions). As toddlers become more social, it is important to help the child use a form that will enable him to interact with his peers even if the form is not spoken speech.
- The ultimate goal for any child is to learn to communicate because it is meaningful to him. You want the child with special needs to learn to do more than just tell you what he wants and needs; you want him to learn to use communication as a form of self-expression.

In addition to these general guidelines, the following are some communication strategies that may help a child with special needs practice his developing communication skills:

- "Nothing is free." Require the child to show you what he wants by pointing, gesturing, or using sign language. Even if he is unable to tell you what he wants, make an effort to encourage him to "show" you.
- Encourage reciprocity in everything you do with the child. Play simple games that involve taking turns, such as rolling a ball back and forth between you and the child. When playing, verbalize what you are doing. Say, "It is my turn," and point to yourself, then say, "It is your turn," and point to the child.
- Consistently respond to every communication attempt, even if it is unintentional. Verbalize what the child is doing and assume that he understands you.
- Start an activity, then stop, and try to get the child to request "more," either by moving his body, putting his hands together to make the sign for "more," or by looking at you.
- Respond to any initiation of a communication interaction by the child and build on his expanding vocabulary by giving him experiences that will help him develop new words. If he is using pictures to communicate, encourage him to use words, too.
- Throughout all stages of communication, the environment plays a major role in helping children interact. Play games where you practice the rules of conversation (such as starting, stopping, and waiting for a turn). Help the child use communication for more than just simple requests; encourage him to communicate feelings or opinions as well.
- Most important, make communicating a fun activity by singing songs, saying rhymes, and reading books to children every day.

Terms Used in This Chapter

articulation—The way words and sounds are pronounced.

augmentative forms of communication—Generally used to describe methods of communication that do not include spoken language. These alternative methods may be electronic or non-electronic such as using picture cards.

communication board—A board or notebook with pictures in it that is used by a child to communicate.

expressive language—Describes how well a child expresses his wants and needs to others.

fetal heart rate test—A test given to measure the heart rate of an infant before birth.

high-tech—A type of technology that requires a battery or is more sophisticated, such as a computer.

intelligibility—How well a child's speech is understood by a listener.

intentional communication—Purposeful and meaningful communication or communication used as a means to get something or gain attention.

language delay—A delay in language due to a circumstance, such as lack of opportunity to learn language or English as a second language.

language disorder—A true language disorder occurs when the child has prolonged language delays not caused by external factors.

language sample—A written sample representing how a child uses language in everyday activities.

low-tech—Assistive technology that is simple to make and usually does not require a battery to operate.

misarticulation—Mispronunciation of words, such as when one sound is substituted for another sound.

picture communication system—Using pictures that enable a child to communicate by pointing to a picture to indicate a want or need.

picture sequence cards—Cards that are placed in order to depict the sequence in which an activity is completed.

receptive language—Refers to what a listener receives and understands from a communication partner.

reflexive crying—When an infant cries to express feelings, but without a specific intention.

Resources Used in This Chapter

Bowen, C. (1998). *Typical speech development: the gradual acquisition of the speech sound system*. Retrieved from www.speech-language-therapy.com/acquisition.html

Fitzpatrick, M. (2002) Theories of child language acquisition. *Linguistic Inquiry* 33(4), 693–705.

Gould, P., & Sullivan, J. (1999). *The inclusive early childhood classroom: Easy ways to adapt learning centers for all children*. Beltsville, MD: Gryphon House.

Prather, E., Hendrick, D., & Kern, C. (1975). Articulation development in children aged two to four years. *Journal of Speech and Hearing Disorders*, 40, 179–191.

Schiller, P. (1999). *Start smart*. Beltsville, MD: Gryphon House.

Singer, D., Golinkoff, R. M., & Hirsh-Pasek, K. (Eds.) (2006). *Play = Learning: How play motivates and enhances children's cognitive and social-emotional growth*. New York: Oxford University Press.

Sussman, F. (1999). *More than words*. Toronto, Canada: Hanen Center.

For More Information

Chen, D., Klein D. M., & Haney. (2000). *Promoting learning through active interaction. A guide to early communication with young children who have multiple disabilities.* Baltimore: Paul H. Brookes.

Johnston, S. S., McDonnell, A. P., Nelson, C., & Magnavito, A. (2003). Teaching functional communication skills using augmentative and alternative communication in inclusive settings. *Journal of Early Intervention.* 25(4), 263–280.

Parette, P., & McMahan, G. A. (2002). What should we expect of assistive technology: Being sensitive to family goals. *Teaching Exceptional Children*, 23(1), 56–61.

Rowland, C. (1996). *Communication matrix. A communication skill assessment for individuals at the earliest stages of communication development.* Portland, OR: Oregon Health Sciences University.

Schiller, P., & Willis, C. (2008). *Inclusive literacy lessons.* Beltsville, MD: Gryphon House.

Cognitive Development and Play

Provide novel objects for the child to explore.

The Infant Brain

There is no time in a child's life when she will have more brain cells than at birth. However, how those cells interconnect to form synapses or "pathways" within the brain is of greater importance than the total number of cells in her brain (Jensen, 2005). This cell activity determines whether the child learns to solve problems and is able to process new information, or whether she struggles with the most basic skills. While there has been a lengthy debate as to whether development is more strongly influenced by

Note

The first time a term is used in this chapter it appears in bold. All terms in bold are defined at the end of this chapter, beginning on page 111.

heredity or the environment, recent brain research has helped show it is a combination of both factors that influence growth and development.

Factors Influencing Brain Development

At birth, some of the "wiring" within the brain is fully functioning, especially those connections within the brain stem. For example, **primitive (involuntary) actions**, which are controlled by the brain, are already functional in a newborn. These primitive reflexes or actions include respiration, heartbeat, and reflexes. Higher functions, (such as those controlled by the cerebral cortex) are still rudimentary, and what happens during the first few years of a child's life will determine the development of those parts of the brain. One way to help infants develop strong connections within the brain is to provide a variety of sensory experiences immediately after birth. Remember, it is never too early to begin stimulating a baby's brain by singing, talking, and rocking her throughout the day.

Key Concepts During the First Year of Life

1. Babies come into the world with a brain that is wired to learn.
2. Experiences during the first years of life help children make the correct and logical connections needed to function and explore novel situations and objects.
3. The cerebral cortex, which is responsible for language and spatial orientation, is dormant at birth; by age one, it is very active.
4. The cognitive skills a child develops are determined by her early experiences as well as her ability to process information and retrieve that information when needed.

Cognitive Skills

Cognitive skills have been given many names—intelligence, problem-solving skills, information processing, and knowledge acquisition skills—to name a few. For this book, cognitive development will be discussed in the context of play, and in terms of:

- Memory;
- Problem solving;
- The ability to compare different situations in order to evaluate their similarities and differences; and
- The mental steps used in processing information.

What Is the Relationship Between Play and Cognitive Skills?

If you research the meaning of cognition, you will find that it is "the act of knowing." The most effective avenue for infants, toddlers, and two-year-olds to develop cognition is within the context of play, which, for most children, is a valuable and fun way to learn. Play helps a child develop relationships with others, learn how to solve problems, express emotions, and use imagination to create new experiences. By exploring her surroundings, the child learns how to take previous knowledge and apply it to a novel situation. There is no single method or product that has a more profound effect on how young children learn about their world than play. It is the main vehicle through which children learn to get along with others and socialize; it is an important way for experimentation and learning to solve problems in the child's everyday world. Play, like other developmental milestones, evolves as the child begins to experience new activities and explore new environments. The **solitary play** of a toddler, with experience, develops into the interactive, **reciprocal play** of a preschool-age child.

The Stages of Play

While the stages of play have been described in many ways, most experts agree that typically developing children begin to explore their environment by manipulating and experimenting with objects that interest them. Solitary play involves the child's internalizing what she learns as she investigates each newly discovered object and the integration of each new activity into her memory. Toward the end of the first year as infants learn about **reciprocity** or give and take, they may begin to play games, such as "peek-a-boo" with an adult. Other types of play may involve the child handing an object to an adult in an effort to get the adult to do something, such as shake the toy, turn on a toy, make a noise with it, or otherwise use the toy to entertain the infant. The next stage is **parallel play**, which occurs when a child plays in close proximity to other children but with no real interaction. The third stage of play is **associative play**, in which two children play side-by-side and may share a few of the same toys, while their goals for the activity remain independent of one another. The final stage of play is **cooperative play**, during which play is organized and focused toward mutual goals, such as when two children share blocks and build a road together for their play cars.

In addition to what they are able to learn through one or more of the stages of play, infants also learn as they become involved in more **functional play**. In other words, the infant becomes intrigued by more than just a moving mobile or a soft toy. As she uses particular objects more frequently, she begins to experiment with them in different ways. For example, she may place one block on top of another or lay the blocks down in a line. She might intentionally put a plastic spoon beside a bowl or attempt to place it in the bowl. As she develops cognitively, she may substitute one object for another (**symbolic play**), as in picking up a block and pretending it is a camera. This will lead to **imaginative play** or **pretend play**. For young children, play should:

- Provide a fun and joyful experience;
- Enable generalization as well as problem-solving skills;
- Require that a child become an active participant;
- Provide a voluntary experience that comes from within;
- Have no real agenda except what the child wants it to be;
- Require that a child learn to be symbolic, such as when a cardboard box becomes a jet plane; and
- Be the primary vehicle through which the child learns the rules of **socialization**.

Infant Play

During the first year of life, infants play by experimenting with body sensations using their senses. In addition, they use movement to help them learn what their bodies can do. Social attachments are made when an infant is held; she begins to match a voice, smile, or facial expression with a specific person. Toys that are appropriate for an infant attract her attention with clear contrasting colors, sounds, or textures. Babies need objects they can grasp, push, or pull to master motor abilities and develop coordination. Suggestions to enhance the play of infants with and without special needs include:

- Hold and sing to young babies. Being held closely and cuddled frequently assists in building the child's self-worth, security, and tactile system. It also

Select toys that the child enjoys and follow his lead.

enables her to feel safer about her world, which will then lead to her being more willing to explore it.

- Rock, sway, and swing your baby gently, to help her acquire a sense of movement and balance. This develops one of the hidden senses, the **vestibular system**, which helps the child learn to balance herself while sitting up or learning to walk.
- Echo the infant's babble. Use different inflections and tones, and do not discount the importance of your facial expressions on her development.
- Provide a variety of play settings for infants with special needs. Include outdoor activities as often as possible. This will expand the infant's world outside of her crib and home.
- Play different kinds of music, such as classical, soft rock, and children's folk music. Don't forget to sing to infants too; they enjoy hearing your voice.
- For newborns, use toys with contrasting colors, such as black, white, and red, which are easier for them to see. As the child gets older, placing brightly colored toys near her will increase her interest and curiosity.
- Provide soft toys (a stuffed animal or soft rattle) for the infant to hold, grasp, and feel. If she doesn't have the motor skills to hold the rattle, you can put your hand over hers and you can hold it together.
- Give babies toys that make noise or light up. Remember, infants with hearing loss or those who are visually impaired will need toys that stimulate their strongest sense. For example, children with hearing impairments are more likely to respond to a brightly colored toy than a toy that makes noises when it is squeezed.
- Provide children with opportunities to experience various smells. These may include the aromas of lemon, vanilla, apple, or natural smells, such as grass or flowers. Learn which smells the child prefers and incorporate them into daily activities.
- Hang large pictures at eye level. These might include pictures of the child's family members, pets, or other animals. Initially, an infant will respond better to pictures without a lot of detail. For example, instead of putting up a picture of a farm, put up a picture of a single farm animal.
- Hang toys over the crib. Motion-activated mobiles are especially fun for the infant because they reinforce her learning about cause and effect.
- Have a clean, safe space for babies to crawl. Put bright toys nearby so babies can reach out for the toys or move toward the toys.
- Place a big cardboard box on the floor so the infant can crawl inside and play.
- Put soft cushions on the floor for the baby to roll and bounce on. Make sure the child is able to roll and has enough head control to avoid getting "stuck" and experience difficulty breathing.
- Read books aloud to infants. Select books that have bright, colorful pages. Babies will respond to the rhythm in your voice. Over time, they will learn that words have meaning and will be able to identify many of the objects she has heard about.

The Play of Toddlers and Twos

Toddler play is usually more sophisticated than infant play. Toddlers frequently engage in parallel play. Some are able to play alone for up to an hour, while most still want adults in close proximity. As toddlers continue to practice and experiment with play, they usually engage more interactively with others, which leads to the development of more sophisticated language skills. Eventually, toddlers and two-year-olds move into a more complex type of play, known as socio-dramatic play or pretend play. While in the initial stages, this type of play is unorganized; the basis for it resides in the child's ability to watch what others do and imitate their play in her play activities. Common characteristics of the play of toddlers and two-year-olds include:

- Beginning to play simple pretend games. Their fantasy play is very short and simple. While it may be a form of parallel play, their play is usually not interactive.
- Sharing is difficult. Toddlers and two-year-olds are generally very self-centered and sharing is difficult. They enjoy playing near other children, but not with other children.

Messy play builds problem-solving skills.

- Asserting themselves by saying "no." This can lead to unsuccessful interactions with other toddlers and two-year-olds.
- Imitating others—Play is often characterized by the imitation of the behavior of adults and others.
- Wanting to help—They often want to help with household tasks, and this can be reflected in their play behavior.
- Easily frustrated—They become frustrated easily; it is imperative that they not be required to play too long with one toy or activity.
- Naturally curious—Because they are more confident than children who are younger than one year old, they are naturally more curious and are more likely to experiment with objects around them.

How Play Evolves

According to Bruce (2004), the initial phase of play involves exploration, during which the infant or toddler will examine, smell, squeeze, and look at a particular toy. In the next phase, the child will attempt to manipulate or investigate the toy in some way. This usually involves investigating the toy to see if it will do anything, such as light up or make noise. In effect, she tries to figure out what the toy is and what it does. It is important to recognize that some toys are very appealing to young children while others do not hold their interest at all. Infants, toddlers, and two-year-olds develop specific preferences very early on. Their interests can often change, meaning that today's preferred toy or activity may be boring to her tomorrow as she moves on to a new toy. The third phase of play involves practice. The more a young child plays (practices) with a toy or object, the more she develops her problem-solving skills. Children with special needs usually require more time and effort to learn a new skill, and will, therefore, need additional practice before they master the skills needed to play with a particular toy. After the child has learned to play with the toy, she moves into the repetition stage, where she will repeat what she has learned about playing with the toy. The more a child repeats an action, the more she learns to use that action. One of the earliest signs that an infant may be intellectually gifted can be noted in how quickly she figures out a novel toy or problem using previously acquired skills.

<table>
<tr><td>The Four
Phases of Play</td></tr>
<tr><td>1. Exploration</td></tr>
<tr><td>2. Investigation</td></tr>
<tr><td>3. Practice</td></tr>
<tr><td>4. Repetition</td></tr>
</table>

Play and Children with Special Needs

Many studies have examined the quality and type of play that young children with special needs will tackle. The classic study by Smilansky (1968) discovered that children with developmental delays (specifically cognitive delays) showed a marked deficit in terms of dramatic play. Other research has shown that, while infants, toddlers, and two-year-olds with special needs can and do play, it is often solitary play. However, as these children move toward parallel play, they have more opportunities for interaction with others. The research clearly shows that simply placing a child with special needs in close proximity to other children will not necessarily mean that interaction will occur. For this reason, you may need to be intentional in how you encourage children with special needs to play.

What Can I Do to Encourage Children to Play?

Before you can encourage play, it is important to spend some time observing the child. Use Table 8–1 to record your observations, which will help you determine what attracts the child most. Structuring play around her interests will not only greatly increase the chances of positive play interactions, but will also make her more likely to show an interest in what goes on in her surroundings.

Play provides multiple opportunities for cognitive development.

Table 8-1 *Play Observations*

Questions to Ask	How Does the Child Play?	Examples You Observe
Does she prefer a toy or an object?	• What does she do with it? • Does she play? • Does she watch while it moves? • Does she sit and stare at the object?	
What activity does she seem to repeat?	• How does she act when she is repeating the activity? • Does it have more than one step? • Will she let others engage in the activity with her?	
What materials does she use most often?	• Is her preference for color or size? • Does she prefer one texture over another? • How does she respond when you introduce something new, such as a new toy?	
What does she do when she plays with an object or toy?	• Will she engage in multiple activities with the same toy? • Will she let others share the toy with her? • Does she play appropriately with the toy or does she carry out a movement repeatedly?	
Will she attempt to explore a novel toy?	• Will she put aside her desired object when something new is introduced? • How does she react to a new toy?	
If she does engage in pretend play, is there a theme she prefers?	• Does she use the same theme (pretending she is a doctor or a firefighter) every time she plays? • Will she assign themes to other activities?	
Does she play with others?	• If she plays with others, whom does she play with most? • Will she play with other children or only adults? • How does she react when you bring over a new peer buddy (see page 107) to play with her?	

Teaching Infants, Toddlers, and Twos with Special Needs

How Do I Use What I Have Observed?

Once you have observed how a child plays and what she prefers to play with, it will be easier to plan activities that focus on her interests. Make sure the child has time to play with preferred objects and is not under stress to stop or share the toy until she is ready. When the child has played with the preferred item for a few minutes, encourage her to try something new by putting the new toy beside her and walking away. Do not take away the preferred toy. After a few minutes, return and ask if she would like to play with the new toy. Another way to help teach the child to play with others is to ask a peer to help. It is important, however, that you select a peer buddy who recognizes that, while the child is different in the way she responds, it can still be fun to play with her.

Water play encourages cognitive development.

How Do I Select an Appropriate Peer Buddy?

A **peer buddy** is a volunteer who agrees to play with the child for a period of time. Observe the children in your class and try to determine who has interests that are similar to that of the child with special needs. Next, look at individual characteristics. Which child might be more tolerant of a peer with special needs? Who seems to be more patient with others? Who might be willing to play with the child, even if the child has rejected her as a friend in the past?

Sometimes, you will be able to identify a peer buddy immediately and can begin to train her in the procedures you have set up for the child. At other times, you may have to be more creative and look outside your classroom for a peer buddy. Maybe there is an older child in another classroom who can visit your class and be a peer buddy for a little while each day. If your program has after-school care, there may be a school-age child who is willing to help out by playing with the child. Some teachers put "help wanted" posters in their classrooms and ask older preschoolers to "apply" for classroom jobs.

If you put up a help-wanted poster for a peer buddy, be sure to put up other help wanted posters for other classroom jobs, so that all children in the class have the opportunity to apply for a classroom position or job. This technique is also very effective for children with special needs, as they can also learn to apply for a classroom job that interests them. Once you have selected the right peer buddy, you can begin helping the toddler or two-year-old with special needs play more effectively with others.

How Do I Begin to Teach the Peer Buddy Process?

Begin the process by talking with the peer buddy and telling her that for the next few days, you would like her to play with the child with special needs. Remember to use the child's name, such as, "Kimberly, thank you so much for volunteering to be a peer buddy for Brandon. Every day I will tell you what I need for you to do to help Brandon learn to play." When selecting a peer buddy for older infants and young toddlers, you should be less directive. In this case, make note of who plays near the child with special needs or select a classmate who you think would be willing to play with her for a short time. Remember, this is an experiment, and every good researcher knows that when something is not working, it is best to stop and try again at another time.

Next, invite the peer buddy to play beside the child for a few minutes. Do not encourage them to play together or communicate. If that happens, great! But, at this point, your goal is to get the child with special needs to accept someone else in her space. She must be willing to do this, before any type of cooperative play is possible. While you may not be able to teach a child with special needs to make friends in the traditional sense, you may be able to orchestrate some situations that encourage positive interactions. However, first, you must teach her to tolerate the presence of other children.

When a child with special needs is able to accept the presence of others in her **personal space**, it is an important step in her learning to play with peers. Because toddlers and two-year-olds tend to be very egocentric, this process will take time, patience, and practice. It is important to know the developmental age as well as the stage (play phase) at which the child is functioning. Some children with special needs are not developmentally able to interact with others while they play.

After the peer buddy has played in the child's space for a few minutes, ask her to leave the area. It is important to gradually introduce children with special needs to the presence of others. Later in the day (or the following day), ask the same peer to help again. This time, encourage her to play beside her friend with special needs for a little longer. Continue this process for several days, before you start encouraging the two children to share their toys. After the child has learned to tolerate a peer and share her toys, it is time to gradually introduce activities that encourage the children to interact.

If the child can communicate with simple signs or uses a communication device, teach the peer buddy how to talk to the child using that form of communication. Even if it is nothing more than making the sign for "want" or "more," it can be the first step to a positive play experience for both children.

Ideas and Activities that Encourage Children to Play

When trying to encourage a child with special needs to play, keep these points in mind:

- Focus on the interests of the child.
- Make interactions with others as natural as possible.
- Recognize that children with special needs may have difficulty adjusting to new play situations and new play materials.
- Explain activities that involve more than one step, providing picture cues to help the child know what to do next.
- Allow the child to leave a play activity if it becomes too overwhelming.
- Honor the child's need to play alone; some children with special needs are not ready to play in large groups.
- Avoid upsetting the child. Let her know in advance that it will soon be time to stop playing, so she has time to accept that there will be a change.

General Suggestions for Teaching Play Strategies

Before selecting a strategy to encourage play, it is important to remember these general suggestions:

- Introduce one new toy or activity at a time. Too much change can be overwhelming. Table 8–2 shows various toys and their uses.
- When teaching the child to do something for the first time, break it down into a few simple steps. Show her each step and then ask her to repeat it.
- Begin with very short periods of structured play. Then, extend the time as the child learns to tolerate the activity.

Table 8–2 *Toys and Their Uses*

Type and General Purpose of Toy	Examples
Toys that encourage cause-and-effect exploration or toys that require an action by the child, such as pushing a button or pulling a lever	• Jack-in-the-Box • Flashlight • Simple switch-operated toys like a tape recorder • See-N-Say toys
Toys that are related to visual-spatial needs	• Puzzles with knobs • Stacking rings • Nesting cups • Shape-sorting toys
Toys that aid in construction or building	• Blocks of various shapes and sizes • Building toys, such as Legos • Stringing beads • Snap-together toys
Toys that encourage reciprocity (an exchange between two people)	• Small hand-held toys • Blowing bubbles • Small moving toys, such as cars, trucks, and airplanes
Sensory toys that encourage creativity	• Art materials, paint, glue, scraps of cloth or paper, art paper, and crayons • String or yarn
"Let's pretend" toys	• Puppets • Realistic-looking toys that represent things, such as food, clothes, and so on • Dress-up clothes, including hats, shoes, and jewelry

- Talk about the activity. Be animated, and use a happy approach by saying things such as, "Wow, I just love rolling the ball to you!" or "You built that tower so high!", "Isn't this fun?"
- When teaching a new skill, use the child's name and tell her what will happen. Then model the steps in the activity and encourage the child to try the activity on her own.
- Make sure every play activity is fun and rewarding for the child. Remember, the main reason children play is because it is fun!

Terms Used in This Chapter

associative play—Play in which two children play side-by-side and may share a few of the same toys while their goals for the activity remain independent of one another.

cognitive skills—Also called intellectual skills or problem-solving skills, refer to "the act of knowing."

cooperative play—Play that is organized and focused toward mutual goals, such as when two children share blocks and build a road together for their play cars.

dramatic or pretend play—Play that involves make believe or acting out a story.

functional play—Play that is meaningful and serves some purpose or function.

imaginative (pretend) play—Play activities that involve using imagination.

parallel play—A type of play in which one child plays near or beside another. Although they may share some of the same toys, they do not play together in a reciprocal fashion.

peer buddy—A peer who serves as a tutor or helper for another child and who is assigned to interact and play with a child for a given time.

personal space—The space in which someone feels comfortable—their comfort zone.

primitive (involuntary) actions—Reflexes or actions controlled by the brain that are already functional in a newborn. These primitive reflexes or actions include respiration, heartbeat, and reflexes.

reciprocal play—Direct play with a partner, when the children interact with each other.

reciprocity—The process of sharing or give and take in which one child completes an action and waits for another child to do something in return, such as when two children roll a ball back and forth to each other.

socialization—The ability to get along with others.

solitary play—Playing alone or play that does not involve others.

symbolic play—Using one object or toy to represent another, such as pretending a square block is a camera or that a cardboard box is a jet plane.

vestibular system—The system in the body that helps the child learn to balance while sitting up or learning to walk.

Resources Used in This Chapter

Bruce, T. (2004). "Play Matters" in Abbott, L., & Langston, A. (eds). *Birth to three matters: Supporting the framework of effective practice.* Berkshire, UK: Open University Press.

Jensen, E. (2005). *Teaching with the brain in mind (2nd ed.).* Alexandria, VA: Association for Supervision and Curriculum Development.

Puckett, M. B., Black, J. K., & Moriarity, J. (2007). *Understanding infant development.* St. Paul, MN: Redleaf Press.

Puckett, M. B., Black, J. K., & Moriarity, J. (2007). *Understanding toddler development.* St. Paul, MN: Redleaf Press.

Singer, D. G., Golinkoff, R. M., & Hirsh-Pasek, K. (2006). *Play = learning: How play motivates and enhances children's cognitive and social-emotional growth.* Oxford, NY: Oxford University Press.

Smilansky, S. (1968). *The effects of sociodramatic play on disadvantaged preschool children.* New York: Wiley.

Willis, C. (2009). *Creating inclusive learning environments for young children.* Thousand Oaks, CA: Corwin Press.

For More Information

Honig, A. (2007). Play: Ten power boosts for children's early learning. *Young Children,* 62(5), 72–78.

Howes, C., Burchinal, M., Pianta, R., Bryant, D., Early, D., Clifford, R., et al. (2008). Ready to learn? Children's pre-academic achievement in pre-kindergarten programs. *Early Childhood Research Quarterly,* 23(1), 27–50.

Kern, P., & Wakeford, L. (2007). Supporting outdoor play for young children: The zone model of playground supervision. *Young Children,* 62(5), 12–18.

Schiller, P. B., & Willis, C. (2008). *Inclusive literacy lessons for early childhood.* Beltsville, MD: Gryphon House.

Simcock, G., & Dooley, M. (2007). Generalization of learning from picture books to novel test conditions by 18- and 24-month-old children. *Developmental Psychology,* 43(6), 1568–578.

Social Competence

Parallel play can be a first step toward developing social skills.

Developing Social Skills

Infants, toddlers, and two-year-olds are social beings; they learn about the world by interacting with other people in that world. **Social competences**, or social skills, are those activities that allow a child to behave in a socially appropriate manner in a variety of different settings. Social skills are what a young child will ultimately use to make friends, interact with adults, and adapt to new environments. For children with special needs, social skills (or the lack of them) can impact how their peers perceive them, how adults in their world treat them, and what they learn about being part of a community at large (Willis, 2009). For this book, social skills will be defined as those that are necessary for:

- Involvement in play situations that involve interaction with others,
- Making and keeping friends, and
- Daily skills needed to function in the early childhood environment, such as taking turns, appropriate behavior, and participation in social encounters.

Note

The first time a term is used in this chapter it appears in bold. All terms in bold are defined at the end of this chapter, beginning on page 121.

Social Skills Development Begins in Infancy

As discussed in Chapter 2, an infant's first experiences with socialization may occur with a parent or caregiver. Research has shown that an infant with special needs may not have the same opportunities for socialization as a typically developing child. This may be a result of his specific medical needs. It could also be because his caregiver is not sure how to interact with him because he does not respond in a traditional manner to attempts at interaction. Regardless of a child's special needs, the foundation for interaction is established when the adults in his world consistently respond to his needs. Interaction with all infants, especially those with special needs, should include:

- *Turn-taking and reciprocity.* This means playing games like Peek-a-Boo and Pat-a-Cake. For a child with significant special needs, this may mean simply rocking her, then stopping to see if he will "ask" for more by slightly moving his body. When you respond to that slight movement with additional rocking and a comment, such as, "Oh you want me to rock you again!" it provides reinforcement, and the infant soon learns that even if he cannot communicate verbally, he can communicate non-verbally with body movement.
- *Frequent communication.* Talk, talk, talk. Infants understand language long before they use it, so continually communicate with them. Describe what you are doing, say a silly rhyme, or just hum softly.
- *Body language that indicates pleasure and satisfaction.* Just as you learn to "read" and "react" to an infant's body language, the same is true of him learning to read you. Through engagement, he can learn to read your actions, as when you are happy to help him and when you seem inconvenienced by his demands.
- *Stimulation, such as rocking, singing, and reading.* Infants need the stimulation of all their senses, and it is never too early to begin reading to them. In fact, research shows that infants and young children who are read to have a better chance of being good readers when they grow up.

How Special Needs Have an Impact on Social Development

To achieve positive interaction goals, you must understand the developmental needs of the child as well as how his special needs may have an impact on his social development. Some ways in which you can achieve these goals include:

- Interact with the child in the context of everyday routines, such as while you are changing a diaper or feeding him. Encourage him to participate in the interaction even if it is only partial participation. For example, place his hand on the spoon and encourage him to help you feed him. To cue a child with a vision impairment that it is time to eat, place a plastic spoon in his hand before you start to feed him. In time, he will learn that the spoon placed in his hand is a cue or prompt that it is "Time to eat!"

- An infant needs opportunities to practice in authentic social settings. Place your hands around the infant's hands and help him clap. You may say something like, "Clap, clap, clap, happy as can be; clap, clap, clap, look at me!" Stop, pick up a small hand mirror, and hold it up for the child to see himself. Before long, the infant will learn to recognize this as the Clap-and-See Game, and anticipate playing it with you by smiling, rocking his body, or attempting to clap on his own.

- Talk to the child and describe what you are doing. Many times, adults like to talk to infants in a high-pitched "baby-talk" voice. While funny voices can be fun for songs and occasional activities, it is very important that children with special needs hear normal adult voices, so they can learn to imitate language in a "true" manner.

- Remember to wait to see if the child responds to you when you talk or gesture to him. His response is an indication that he can "read" your actions (especially the non-verbal cues). For example, when you feed the infant and he pushes away from you, wait to see if he will also let you know he is finished by continuing to turn his body away from the bottle or spoon. Respond by saying, "Oh you are all finished!" Sign the word "finished" by placing your palms together then moving them outward.

- Work closely with the child's family so you know what his interests are as well as what types of music or books he enjoys.

- Teach reciprocity through simple games, such as rolling a ball back and forth or playing with a toy car. Roll the car toward the child and encourage him to roll it back to you.

- Model what you want the infant to do. Be patient, remembering that children with special needs often take a little longer to process information than their peers.

- Imitate actions and sounds. Repeat what the child says and does.

- Keep your body language upbeat and enthusiastic. If you are bored by an activity, a child will be too!

- Have high expectations. Do not assume that, because a child has special needs, he cannot interact with others.

Social Competence

Interacting with Peers

Sometimes when toddlers and two-year-olds interact with each other, it occurs in a negative context. For example, Michael is building with blocks and William wants to join him. William may walk up to Michael and pick up a block. If Michael is opposed to the idea, he may shove William and grab the block out of his hand. In turn, William may scream loudly to protest having his block taken away. These children just had a social interaction. Unfortunately, it was a negative social interaction. To plan positive social interactions, it is important to recognize the relationship between form and function. In other words, you must know how and why a child interacts in a certain way. Bailey and Wolery (1992) note that peer interactions in young children usually take place in these forms:

Expressing affection for a peer is an important social skill.

- Making vocalizations,
- Using proximity (approaching or getting near a peer),
- Touching,
- Giving a toy or other material to a peer,
- Receiving a toy or other material from another child, and
- Looking or making eye contact.

They list these as primary functions or reasons for the interactions:

- Getting another child's attention,
- Initiating interactions,
- Responding to the initiation of others,
- Sustaining an interaction, and
- Ending an interaction to move on to something else.

Of course, for the most part, younger toddlers are not socially competent beings. For example, they cannot consider the form or the function that another child may be using. Because of the egocentric nature of "toddlerhood," most toddlers are unable or unwilling to see beyond their own immediate needs. As they mature and experience more positive interactions with others, typically developing toddlers and two-year-olds learn to participate in more complex social interactions. They learn that if one form or type of interaction does not work, perhaps a different one may be more successful.

As toddlers and two-year-olds develop a larger and more complex repertoire of social skills, they learn to apply their skills to various social contexts. For example, April calls out to Brandy, who gives no response. April may then move closer to Brandy, in an effort to get her attention. If that does not work, April may walk up and touch Brandy on the shoulder. If April is socially competent, she will try a few more times to get Brandy's attention. If there is still no response, April will recognize that Brandy is not interested in playing with her and move on to someone or something else. This comprehension of the nuance of social interaction is something young children usually learn by trial and error, watching others interact, and applying their knowledge to their encounters. For a variety of reasons, children with special needs do not always learn about social interactions by observation and trial and error. They must receive explicit instruction to know when and how to best respond in a social context.

General Socialization Goals for Infants

For infants to be able to:

1. Initiate social interactions to engage the attention of an adult (or another child) for the purposes of socialization.
2. Enter into a play situation that involves one initiation and one response.
3. Understand the concept of reciprocity as it relates to socialization.

Special Needs Issues

For the most part, infants with special needs develop much like their typically developing peers, with the exception that their social development may occur more slowly and that it may take them more time to learn new concepts. There are, however, a few specific special needs that may require extra adaptations for the development of social skills, including:

- *Medically Fragile*: Because of a child's chronic medical needs, you may forget to stop and make eye contact with him or take time to encourage him to interact with other children. For children whose medical needs keep them isolated from others, it is important to provide opportunities where they can interact with other young children.
- *Vision Impaired*: To become familiar with you, an infant with visual impairments may need to touch your face (the same is true when the child is also getting to know others). Lean in closely, and place the child's hand on your face. This will encourage him to learn how to recognize you by touch. Remember, always tell the child what you are going to do before you touch him or pick him up.
- *Hearing Impaired*: Make sure the child can see you while you talk to him. Use touch cues, such as a tap on the arm, to let him know that you are going to pick him up.

- *General Developmental Delays*: Because it takes the infant with a developmental delay longer to learn and master new skills, look for ways to help him practice things, such as waving bye-bye, maintaining eye contact, and attempting a new activity, even if it appears challenging to him. For an infant who resists trying new things or exploring new toys, try working with him using the **hand-over-hand technique,** as this may encourage him to explore something new with more confidence.
- *Motor Development*: Children with motor delays should always be positioned in such a way that they can see what is going on around them. For a child with poor head control, place your hand on the back of his neck, to help stabilize his head, and help him hold his head upright. This will allow eye contact to be established more easily and maintained throughout an interaction.

Social Skills for Toddlers and Twos

During the second year of life, an infant becomes increasingly more sophisticated in social engagement. Social skills for toddlers and two-year-olds include:

- Making friends,
- Taking turns,
- Learning simple rules, and
- Participating in a play group or small group activity.

Strategies for Helping Toddlers and Twos with Special Needs

1. *Making Friends*: A child must learn to interact with others in a social setting to achieve a goal, such as getting what he wants or establishing reciprocity. For example, Clarence has learned that if he grabs for another child's toy, he is likely to be hit or pushed away. Therefore, after he has found this approach unsuccessful, he will try an alternative method when a peer has a toy he wants.

   Friendship skills are especially important for children with developmental delays, because of their limited skills to generalize information. While a typically developing child may relate a social skill that was successful in one setting to another similar setting, it is much more difficult for a child with special needs to be able to do this. Instead, the child with special needs may repeatedly try to solve a problem the same way, even if he has had no previous success. For example, Clarice, a two-year-old with Down syndrome, may use the same method to take possession of a desired toy, which is being held by another child, even though every time she grabs for it, she is hit or pushed away. Further, she may attempt to use the same method in similar situations, having been unable to discover a better way. For that reason, it is crucial for children with special needs to have intensive and intentional instruction about how to handle each social situation. They also need multiple opportunities to practice new social skills by using one or more of these techniques:

- Peer modeling,
- Picture cards to depict positive social interaction, or
- Direct intervention by an adult.

2. *Taking Turns*: Let's face it—no one likes to wait for a turn. However, learning to wait is an important life skill for every child. Facilitate this learning process in children with special needs by redirecting their attention to another activity while they wait, teaching them to ask for a turn, or minimizing the waiting time. This is not to say that a child with special needs should always be first in line. However, if you know that he experiences difficulty in waiting situations, consider putting him second or third in line. While learning to be last is hard for a typically developing child, it is especially difficult for a child with special needs.

3. *Learning Simple Rules*: Whether your classroom rules are depicted by pictures on the wall or set forth by gentle verbal reminders, children with special needs will need extra instruction in learning rules.

4. *Participating in a Play Group or Small Group Activity*: Group activities can be overwhelming for some children, especially those with behavior issues and those with autism. Make sure the child knows what will happen next, and plan short periods of group instruction. Provide opportunities to sing, move around, and interact with others, as sitting for a long time is very challenging for most young children and is often impossible for a young child with special needs.

Social competence involves working and playing with others.

Techniques That Build Social Interaction Skills for Toddlers and Twos

According to Barbara Lowenthal (1996), there are several techniques that can help children with special needs develop socially:

- Arrange the environment so there is enough room to move around and plenty of materials and toys to share. It is also important for the setting to invite children to interact. For example, in the literacy area, you could include a child-sized couch for two, which would allow peers to enjoy looking at a book together.
- Group-affection activities are helpful because affiliation with and acceptance by others is critical for toddlers and two-year-olds. It is important to plan activities that encourage a sense of belonging, such as having the class say welcome chants and sing welcome songs.
- Imitation of peers is a recommended technique. Watching others is an important way for a child to learn. Give him opportunities to imitate his peers.
- Prompts are very helpful. Learn to anticipate how a child may respond in a given situation and prompt the child accordingly. For example, if Lindsey gets upset when you tell her to put away the toys, give her a prompt or gentle reminder a few minutes before it is time to clean up. This provides an opportunity for her to get ready for the transition.
- Reinforcement from you is the strongest feedback a child with special needs can receive. It can be a smile, a pat on the back, or a hug.
- **Correspondence training** involves the child making a statement, such as, "I will stop hitting," and you reinforcing his behavior.
- Peer-mediated interventions are those in which a peer serves as a model.

Summary

To help infants, toddlers, and two-year-olds learn social competence, it is important to structure the children's surroundings for success. The following environmental modifications will be especially helpful for young children with special needs:

1. Keep group sizes small to help promote positive interactions.
2. Provide materials that are appropriate to the age and stage of the child's development.
3. Intentionally plan activities that incorporate collaboration.

Peers can be great social models for children with special needs. They can model social skills, initiate communication interactions, and serve as peer buddies to help a child with special needs complete an activity or work on a developing skill.

Terms Used in This Chapter

correspondence training—A technique in which the child verbally states a behavior that he will or will not do, and you reinforce it.

hand-over-hand technique—A process in which an adult places her hands over the child's hand to guide the child in completion of a task. This serves as a model for the child to promote more independence in the future.

medically fragile—Used to designate a child with chronic medical needs.

reciprocity—Understanding the back-and-forth or give-and-take in an interaction. For example, first I talk to you, then I wait for you to respond to me.

social competence—The skills needed to interact and communicate effectively with others.

Resources Used in This Chapter

Bailey, D. B., & Wolery, M. (1992). *Teaching infants and preschoolers with disabilities.* Upper Saddle River, NJ: Merrill.

Lowenthal, B. (1996). Teaching social skills to preschoolers with special needs. *Childhood Education,* (3)72, 137–141.

Puckett, M. B., & Black, J. K. (2008). *Understanding toddler development.* St. Paul, MN: Redleaf Press.

Willis, C. (2009). *Creating inclusive learning environments for young children.* Thousand Oaks, CA: Corwin Press.

For More Information

Carpenter, M., Pennington, B. F., & Rogers, S. J. (2002). Interrelations among social-cognitive skills in young children with autism. *Journal of Autism and Developmental Disorders,* 32(2), 91–98.

Celeste, M. (2007). Social skills intervention for a child who is blind. *Journal of Visual Impairment & Blindness,* 101(9), 521–533.

McHenry, J. D., & Buerk, K. J. (2008). Infants and toddlers meet the natural world. *Young Children,* 63(1), 40–41.

Patael, S., & Diesendruck, G. (2008). Intentions help children learn meaningful rules. *Journal of Child Language,* 35(1), 221–234.

Rao, P. A., Beidel, D. C., & Murray, M. J. (2008). Social skills interventions for children with Asperger's syndrome or high-functioning autism: A review and recommendations. *Journal of Autism and Developmental Disorders,* 38(2), 353–361.

Motor Development 10

Waving is both a motor skill and a communication skill.

As infants begin to engage with their caregivers, they also learn to explore and engage with their world. For example, they may discover that, when they wave their hands and stretch out their bodies, the brightly-colored mobile above them moves. Initially, these motor movements are experimental; yet their movements become more purposeful and intentional as they develop. Grasping an object with their whole hand and bringing both hands to midline are the types of motor movements infants exhibit as they discover the world around them. Motor development has a profound influence on all other areas of development.

Atypical Motor Development

Causes of Atypical Motor Development

According to Goswami (2004), **atypical motor development** can occur for many reasons, such as brain damage, which occurs before or during birth, orthopedic problems, genetic defects, developmental delays, and sensory impairments. Problems in muscle development are usually grouped in one of these categories:

- Muscle tone,
- Muscle control, or
- Muscle strength.

— Note —

The first time a term is used in this chapter it appears in bold. All terms in bold are defined at the end of this chapter, beginning on page 137.

Muscle Tone

Muscle tone is generally defined as the degree of tension in the muscle when that muscle is at rest. While the body is at rest, unconscious nerve impulses maintain muscles in a partially contracted state. If a sudden pull or stretch occurs, the body responds by automatically increasing the muscle's tension; this reflex helps maintain balance. Generally speaking, there are three types of muscle tone that result in a child's having atypical motor development (Martin, 2006):

1. **Hypotonic** or low muscle tone in which the child appears to have a "floppy" or "rag-doll" appearance to her movements. Children who are hypotonic have flaccid muscle tone, especially in shoulders, hips, and ankles. Because it takes so much effort for the child to move her muscles, she becomes fatigued easily, and is usually less physically active than her peers.

2. **Hypertonic**, the opposite of hypotonic, is characterized by muscles that are stiff and rigid. Another term often used interchangeably with hypertonic is spastic. A child who is hypertonic has difficulty with motor movements; her muscles appear to be "locked" in such a way that movement is difficult, especially walking, bending at the knees, or bending the arm at the elbow.

3. A child with a combination of both hypotonic and hypertonic muscle tone is said to have **fluctuating muscle tone**, which results in difficulty with both contracting and relaxing her muscles. When the child's muscles are relaxed, she appears very floppy, but when the child starts to move her muscles, they become hypertonic or rigid and her movements are very jerky and stiff.

Muscle Control and Strength

While some muscle movement is voluntary—meaning, it takes conscious effort—other movements, such as eye blinking, are involuntary. A child who has difficulty controlling her muscles may exhibit involuntary movements over which she has not control. These involuntary movements include:

- Twitches,
- Tremors, and
- Writhing movements.

Involuntary movements usually occur because of fluctuating muscle tone. Sometimes, poor muscle control can result in characteristics such as a child having difficulty opening and closing her mouth or lifting her arms. In extreme cases, a child with very limited muscle control will most likely be confined to a wheelchair and be unable to walk or feed herself.

Muscle strength generally refers to what happens when the nervous system communicates a message to the muscle fibers to contract. Often, the force produced by a muscle contraction is against resistance. A child with strong muscles can pick up blocks, play on an outside climbing toy, run fast, and lift objects over her head; a child with poor muscle strength has difficulty with these activities. Some degenerative conditions, such as **muscular dystrophy**, result in the child's losing muscle strength over a period of time. Spinal cord injuries can also result in loss of muscle strength.

Cerebral Palsy

The most common motor delay or impairment is **cerebral palsy**, which can be caused by many factors. It is a broad term describing neurological disorders that appear in infancy or early childhood and permanently affect body movement and muscle coordination. In other words, cerebral palsy describes a variety of conditions that result in the child having permanent difficulty controlling the movement of her muscles. Unlike conditions like muscular dystrophy, cerebral palsy is not degenerative; it will not get worse as the child gets older. Cerebral palsy is caused by malfunctions in the parts of the brain that control muscle movement.

Most children with cerebral palsy are born with it. However, a small number of children have cerebral palsy as the result of brain damage in the first few months or years of life. Brain infections, such as bacterial meningitis or viral encephalitis; or a head injury resulting from a motor vehicle accident, fall, or child abuse can also result in a diagnosis of cerebral palsy. Common characteristics include:

- Lack of muscle coordination when performing voluntary movements (**ataxia**),
- Stiff or tight muscles with exaggerated or "jerky" movement (**spasticity**),
- Walking with one foot or leg dragging,
- Walking on the toes,
- A crouched gait or a "scissored" walk, and
- Muscle tone that is either too stiff or too floppy.

Fine and Gross Motor Skills

Helping a child with motor challenges usually involves activities that address either gross motor skills or fine motor skills. Gross motor skills refer to the motor or movement activities where the child uses her entire body, such as walking, running, climbing, and jumping. Gross motor skills include:

- Balance—ability to maintain equilibrium and stay upright.
- Body awareness—posture and control of the head.
- Crossing the mid-line—bringing hands or feet across the center of the body.
- Laterality—awareness of the left and right sides of the body.
- Major muscle coordination—movement of the muscles.
- Spatial orientation—awareness of the body position in space and in relation to other objects or people.

Provide opportunities for children to practice newly acquired motor skills.

Fine motor skills are those activities involving the fingers, hands, and arms; these also include eye-hand coordination. Activities involving fine motor skill development include grasping a pencil, cutting with scissors, stringing beads, and picking up small objects. It is important to remember that, while major milestones, such as sitting up, crawling, walking, and so on, are certainly important, they are only achieved when the child has opportunities to learn the smaller, less noticeable, motor skills that contribute to her ability to perform those skills.

Primary Coordination—The Infant Begins to Coordinate Her Muscles

Head Control

The first, and perhaps most important, milestone that an infant acquires is head control. Head control allows the infant to hold her head up so she can see what is going on around her and track people and objects. These are simple techniques that caregivers can use to help a child develop head control:

- Place the baby face down on a mat or quilt and put a favorite doll or toy directly in front of him. Encourage the child to lift her head, in an attempt to look at the toy. If the child is unable to lift her head, place one hand on her chin and another on her neck, to help support her.
- Lie on your back on the floor with the child face-down on your stomach. Make a funny face or talk softly to the child. Watch to see if she attempts to lift her head to look at your face. If she is unable to do so, place both your hands gently around the baby's ribcage and slowly lift her up so she can see your face. Place the baby back on your stomach and continue the activity until the child seems tired or bored.
- Place the baby on her stomach on a thick blanket. Mirror that position with your own body until you are eye level with the child. Talk gently to her and tell her you are going to take her for a ride. Stand up and slowly pull the blanket across the floor to encourage head control and overall balance as the child enjoys a fun ride.
- After the child has enough control to hold her head up, use a large ball (beach-ball size) to strengthen this new skill. Place the child on the ball and, holding her securely with both hands, rock her back and forth. Most infants enjoy the gentle rocking and hold up their heads while they rock. This activity helps the child further develop head control.
- As the infant gains even more strength and can hold her head up for a longer time, sit with her on the floor and gently take her hands. Play a see-saw game, pulling her gently to a sitting position while holding her hands. Sing, talk softly, or make funny faces. The child will enjoy watching you from different positions as you help her sit up.

Teaching Infants, Toddlers, and Twos with Special Needs

Place a toy just outside the child's reach and then encourage him to crawl to it.

Kicking

When an infant is placed on her back, she has a natural inclination to kick her legs back and forth. At first, the kicking is very sporadic and uncoordinated, but as the child practices, it becomes more intentional and organized. With additional practice, the kicking may become rhythmic as if the child is peddling an invisible tricycle. Kicking helps the infant learn about how her body is located in space. Suggestions to help a child with special needs practice kicking include:

- Place the baby on the floor and turn on music. Try varying the tempo and style to see if the child coordinates her kicking movements in time to the music.
- If the child has difficulty kicking, place your hands on her ankles, alternating lifting each in time to the music. This gives her the sensation of kicking her legs. Stop and see if the child will attempt to kick her legs without your help. Remember to reinforce every attempt. Continue the game until the child grows tired or bored with the activity.
- Use bath time as an opportunity to practice kicking. Gently, hold the child by the waist and place her in a tub or small swimming pool. The buoyancy of the water will help the child as she begins to kick her legs back and forth.

- Place two chairs about one foot apart. Tie a ribbon or string between the two chairs. Attach elastic to a small brightly colored toy or set of jingle bells and then attach the toy or bells to the string. Place the baby under the toys and encourage her to use her feet to make the toys move. If the child does not attempt the activity, use your hands to demonstrate what will happen when the toy is moved. For some children with motor challenges, it may be necessary for you to use your hands to help her kick the objects dangling overhead.
- With the infant lying on her back, place your palms on the bottom of her feet. See if she will attempt to kick, pushing against your palms.

Hands and Arms

Hands and arms are used for a variety of motor skills, including grasping an object, holding a spoon, and, later, holding a crayon or pencil. Later, infants learn to thrust their arms forward when playing and eventually will reach their arms out as if to say, "Pick me up!" Babies use their hands to help explore new and novel toys and play reciprocal games, such as rolling a ball or making a toy move. Table 10–1 includes suggestions for specific types of special needs. Activities that encourage hand movements include:

Look for ways to help children practice walking.

- Place your finger on the child's palm. She will close her hand around your finger. Initially, this response is nothing more than a reflex; as you react responsively to the child, she soon learns it is a game. When she closes her fist around your finger, remember to smile, laugh, and encourage her to continue.
- Once the child has learned to close her hand around your finger, replace your finger with objects of varying textures and sizes. Small balls that light up when squeezed can be very entertaining for an infant, which also reinforces the all-important concept of cause and effect.
- Sit on the floor with the child sitting or leaning against your chest, facing outward. Reach around the infant and take her hands in yours. Sing a song, while moving her hands back and forth. Remember to cross her midline often, as this not only improves muscle control but it also helps brain development.
- After a child has learned to grasp an object, help her transfer it from hand to hand. Once again, objects that light up or make noise when moved can be very motivating for a child.
- Place an object slightly out of reach and see if the child attempts to reach for it. If she attempts the movement, give her the toy, even if she is unable to reach it. This activity reinforces her effort and encourages the infant to keep trying.

- Clapping is an important hand movement. Sit on the floor. Using your chest for support, help the infant sit facing forward. Put your hands over hers and clap together to a favorite song. Stop and see if the child will reach out for you to continue. When the child reaches for you, remember to say, "Great, you want more clapping."

Table 10-1 *Suggestions for Specific Types of Special Needs*

Special Need	Suggestions
Visual Impairments	<ul><li>Use objects that make noise, when playing with the child.</li><li>Children with visual challenges learn early to track sound. Remember to talk with her when you are beginning an interaction.</li><li>If the child has some residual vision (usable vision), be sure to position her so she can see your face and watch what you do.</li></ul>
Hearing Impairments	<ul><li>Every time you approach the child, call her name in a loud, clear voice.</li><li>Use brightly colored objects or toys that light up to encourage interaction.</li><li>Place the child against your shoulder so she can look behind you. Walk around and introduce her to new sites and people.</li><li>Use brightly colored ribbon to hang down in a mobile above the child's head. As she kicks her feet, the ribbons will flutter back and forth.</li><li>Make a bracelet of jingle bells to use when you practice clapping, the additional noise will help the child use her residual hearing.</li></ul>
Physical Challenges	<ul><li>Sudden movements may startle the child, causing her muscles to contract or stiffen. Move slowly and tell her before you lift her.</li><li>For a child with stiff or rigid legs, avoid trying to force her legs to bend. Instead, massage her legs gently, helping the child relax.</li><li>For a child with severe motor challenges, it is important that she sit upright. Position the child with support from your body so she can sit upright.</li><li>If a child has no head control, sit her on your lap facing you. Use one hand to support her back, while the other hand supports her neck. Gently, lift her into an upright sitting position.</li><li>For the bicycling exercise, place a small pillow or soft toy between the child's legs to discourage a scissoring effect.</li><li>Provide multiple opportunities for the child to practice using different sets of muscles. Carry the child facing forward, for example, so that she can see a new set of people and objects.</li><li>A child with tightly clenched fists is unable to grasp. Gently unclench each of her fingers and massage her hands to encourage her to relax.</li><li>Clapping may be very difficult for a child with motor issues. Begin by placing the child's hand in your palm, and interlace your fingers between hers to help her clap.</li></ul>

(Continued)

Table 10–1 *Suggestions for Specific Types of Special Needs (continued)*

Special Need	Suggestions
Cognitive Challenges	• Practice activities often and remember to smile at the child when she is successful. • Children with cognitive challenges may have additional issues. For example, a child with Down syndrome may have both cognitive challenges and muscle issues, which require that you massage her muscles prior to beginning a new motor sequence.
Tactile Defensiveness	• When placing the child on a blanket or mat to practice kicking, experiment with various surfaces to see what type is most comfortable for the child. • It will take some time for a child who has tactile defensiveness to get used to being held. To relax the child, hold her gently in your arms and sway back and forth. • Children with tactile issues may have other sensory integration issues as well. Remember to maintain indirect lighting and monitor the environment for textures, odors, and sounds that may distract her.
Medically Fragile (Chronic Health Issues)	• Make sure the child is positioned in a way that does not compromise any medical equipment she may require. • For a child with chronic health issues, wash your hands and her hands often, and place her on surfaces that are clean and as germ-free as possible.

Sophisticated Movement Patterns

Rolling Over

Once the child has learned to roll over from stomach to back and from back to stomach, her world becomes larger and more interesting. These suggestions can help you provide the child with opportunities to practice the skills necessary to roll over:

- Place the child on her back and gently roll her body from side to side.
- Support the child with one hand on her stomach and one on her back and gently roll her over.
- Sing to the child while rotating her hips from side to side. Try this song, which is sung to the tune of "Row, Row, Row Your Boat":

Roll, roll, roll you go,
Rolling right along.
Rolling front and rolling back,
As we sing a song.

- Use a wedge-shaped pillow or make a slight incline with pillows. Position the child so that her hands will not interfere with rolling over.

Rolling over is one of the earliest motor-coordination skills infants learn.

- Even if a child is unable to roll over, place her on her back, as well as on her stomach for a few minutes, to see if she will attempt to roll over. Reinforce her attempts by supporting her with your hands and helping her roll over.

Sitting Up

Most babies sit up alone by about 7 to 9 months. However, it is important to remember that a child with special needs may progress slower than her peers. Do not be concerned if a child is not sitting up unassisted until much later. Once the infant is able to sit up, she not only has a new and broadened perspective on the world, she is also able to have much more control of her upper body, arms, and hands. To help the child build the muscle control skills needed for sitting up, it may be necessary to initially use supported sitting to help her. Supported sitting includes such things as using your hands to support the child while she sits; placing the child in the corner of a couch or easy chair, or using an adaptive seat, such as a corner chair or adapted highchair. These suggestions may help the child prepare to sit independently:

- Encourage the child to hold up her head while in a seated position. Sit with the child's trunk and head supported. You can sit with her between your legs, placing one hand on her neck and the other hand on her back, to help support her. Invite a co-worker to sit facing the child and gently blow on her forehead or sing softly to her.

Throwing a ball encourages the use of several muscle groups.

- Use a favorite song or a favorite toy to get the child's attention. Hold the toy at eye level to encourage her to hold up her head and look at the toy.
- Gently hold the child's hands in yours and sing a song. Try something like this, which is sung to the tune of "Three Blind Mice":

  I love (use the child's name). *I love* (use the child's name).
  Smiling, playing all day long, singing a silly song.
  I love you! I love you!

Mobility

Creeping and Crawling

Children will creep before they crawl. Creeping is a movement in which the infant uses her arms to drag herself on her stomach across the room. A young child crawls on her hands and knees with her stomach off the floor. Once a child is able to crawl, she is suddenly able to do much more than just look at the world around her. She is now ready to move around from place to place and from activity to activity at her own pace. In order to crawl, a baby must have enough strength and overall coordination of her muscles to push forward with her feet from a prone position. Table 10–2 includes

Table 10–2 *Suggestions for Specific Types of Special Needs*

Special Need	Suggestions
Visual Impairments	• Children lacking the visual cues to help them determine spatial relationships will need extra help with rolling over, crawling, and sitting up. From the beginning, tell the infant exactly what you are going to do before you do it. For example, say, "I am going to help you roll over," before gently rolling the infant from front to back or vice-versa. • After starting each activity, stop momentarily to make sure the child is not getting upset because something is happening to her, as she may not be able to see visual clues. • Use your voice inflection to cue the child about directionality. For example, you could say, "Up" in a high voice and "Down" in a low voice. Practice this by lifting the child up and saying "Up, up, up we go" in a high voice, and bring the child down, by saying "Down, down, down," in a low voice.
Hearing Impairments	• Continue to cue the baby by calling her by name before each activity. • Play music during an activity. Even a child with profound hearing loss can feel the vibrations. • Continue to use brightly colored objects or toys that light up to encourage interaction.
Physical Challenges	• Be sure to work with the child's physical therapist so that you will know which positions work best for her. • Initially, practice activities like holding up her head, sitting, or maintaining head control by placing the child in your lap. This will give her a sense of security. • Remember, you may need to stretch her legs or help her flex her arms, in order for her muscles to be ready for activities.
Cognitive Challenges	• When practicing an activity, such as lifting the head, it may be necessary for you to break it down into small steps. • Children with Down syndrome will need extra practice with balance. Hold the infant in your lap and gently swing her from side to side.

suggestions for specific types of special needs. To encourage crawling, try these activities:

- With one hand, place a favorite toy just out of the child's reach. Encourage the infant to propel herself forward by pushing against your other hand.
- For an infant who is trying to crawl but just cannot get the momentum she needs, encourage her to use your hand to propel herself forward.
- Using a wedge-shaped pillow, make an incline for the child to crawl down. It is easier for her to crawl downhill than on a flat surface.
- Use a surface with traction, such as a textured mat or carpet, as this will keep the infant's knees from slipping.
- To encourage crawling, place the child on all fours and use your hands to gently rock her back and forth.

Before encouraging a "crawling marathon" with the infant, be sure that you have baby-proofed everything in sight. It is easy to underestimate the speed at which a crawling infant can move, so double-check the area. Baby gates and natural boundaries, such as walls, make perfect enclosed environments for an infant to practice crawling.

Pulling Up

Pulling up is a pre-requisite skill for walking. Once a child learns to pull herself up to stand, she is right around the corner from taking that first step. These are some suggestions for encouraging pulling up:

- To help the child pull up, support her trunk by placing one hand loosely around her waist. Then, let her pull up by holding your hand or finger. Do not force the child to pull up, and do not use your strength to pull her up.
- Sometimes, a baby will pull up and get "stuck" in a standing position. If this happens, gently massage the backs of her legs and use your hands to help her sit back down.

Walking

Once an infant learns to walk, the world suddenly becomes very large, and she begins a true period of discovery. For some children, walking will not be an option; they will require devices, such as walkers, wheelchairs, or adaptive crutches to be mobile. Suggestions to encourage walking include:

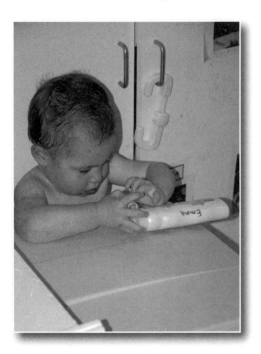

Fine motor skills are best learned in the context of play.

- Most babies will cruise before they walk. **Cruising** is when babies walk while holding on to your hands or objects in the room. Make sure the surfaces are clear and that any obstacles that might cause her to fall have been removed.
- Some babies need props to help them. Encourage walking by allowing the child to push a box or small chair around the floor. Monitor carefully so she will not fall into the chair.
- Hold a brightly colored scarf in one hand and encourage the child to walk holding the other end of the scarf.
- If the child requires a walker or piece of adaptive equipment for mobility, be sure you have collaborated with her physical therapist so you know how and when to use it.

Toddler and Two-Year-Old Skills

In addition to the motor and mobility skills included in this chapter, as the child matures there are additional fine and gross motor skills that she should accomplish in order to be independent. Many of these skills build on previously learned motor skills, and will eventually lead to her to be able to write, throw a ball, and feed herself. Table 10–3 outlines some activities that will help a child build fine and gross motor skills.

Table 10–3 *Activities to Build Motor Skills*

Fine Motor Skills	Gross Motor Skills
Cutting • Select scissors the child can use. There are a variety of adaptive scissors available for children with motor challenges. • Cut for fun using different colored paper and cloth.	**Spatial Relationships** • Teach spatial relationships by helping the child to stand *in front of* a chair or stand *behind* a chair. Remember to verbalize what she is doing. • Practice the same activities with a small box or container and assist the child as she places items *in, on, under,* or *beside* the container. • Model concepts for the child by placing large blocks *in, under, beneath,* and *on top* of each other while describing what you are doing.
Pasting • Use paper, string, yarn, cotton, cloth.	**Throwing** • Practice throwing a ball with two hands. • Practice throwing a ball over her head. • Toss a beanbag back and forth with a friend, moving one step back each time. • Use an empty coffee can to play a beanbag toss game.
Self-Help Skills • Practice buttoning, zipping, and lacing. • Practice opening/closing a jar. • Roll out playdough with a rolling pin.	**Laterality** • Practice activities using her left hand and right hand. • For older toddlers, try modeling and singing the "Hokey-Pokey."
Pre-Writing • Scribble on paper. • Practice connecting the dots.	**Legs/Arms** • Gallop like a horse. • Walk while swinging arms back and forth. • Crawling and pulling up are also good activities for younger toddlers.
	Balance • Trunk movement. • Dance to music. • Sing songs that require movements. • Move like animals—creep, crawl, and gallop.

Positioning and Handling

While movement is important, there are times when the child will not be moving. During those times, it is imperative that her body be placed into positions that optimize her motor skills and help control abnormal reflexes and involuntary movement. The child's physical therapist can help you learn how to position the child for certain daily activities, such as large group time or working in centers. In addition, there are some general positioning and handling techniques that are useful to know. Positioning involves placing the child in a position that stabilizes her body and normalizes muscle tone. Stabilizing a child's trunk for activities that require sitting should allow her to use her arms with more control.

Proper positioning is very important for children with motor issues.

It is important to remember that the position of a child should be as natural as possible and similar to the way other children in the classroom might be positioned. The child should be situated so she can participate in class activities. Keep the child at the same level as other children, as this makes communication and social interaction easier. When an activity is conducted on the floor, position the child on the floor with appropriate support, such as using an adapted chair or the physical support provided by another adult. When carrying the child, try to hold her in a manner that allows her to visually inspect the environment and socialize with others, while helping build her strength. Also, consider the child's choice and preferences when implementing positioning and handling strategies. Allow the child to select positions and areas where she would like to play. Remember to give the child an opportunity to perform as much of the movement as possible for herself.

Handling refers to the way a child is lifted. Generally speaking, when lifting a child, her head should be kept upright and she should be stabilized so that her muscle tone can be as normal as possible. When lifting the child, tell her you plan to lift her and ask her to help in any way possible. Lift the child gently, protecting yourself from back injury by bending your knees and keeping your back straight as you lift.

Adaptive Equipment

Sometimes, a child may require adaptive equipment to stand, sit, or walk. The child's physical therapist will help you learn to position the child in her adaptive device or wheelchair. Adaptive equipment for children with motor issues may include a:

- Wheelchair or walker for getting around in the classroom;
- Prone stander to help the child stand for activities that require standing, such as washing her hands or working at a table; and
- Specialized chair that enables the child to sit with her back straight.

Summary

As an infant becomes more accustomed to using her muscles, she will experiment with combinations, such as hopping or jumping. What starts out as an attempt to pull up in the crib will lead to her being able to pull up, sit down, and pull up again. Remember that it is very important that the child is seated or positioned so she can participate in daily activities as much as possible. Even if she cannot do exactly what other children are doing, she can **partially participate** in activities.

If the child needs adaptive equipment, work closely with her physical therapist to learn how to use the equipment so that it is comfortable for the child and gives her access to what is going on around her. Also, it is important to be sure aisles and classroom areas are wide enough to accommodate a wheelchair or walker. Be creative and think about ways to help the child with motor delays actively engage in activities with peers, keeping in mind that she may tire easily because of the extra effort she expends to use her muscles.

Terms Used in This Chapter

ataxia—A lack of muscle coordination when performing voluntary movements.

atypical motor development—Motor development that does not follow the development observed in other children who are the same chronological age.

cerebral palsy—A broad term used to describe neurological disorders that appear in infancy or early childhood that permanently affect body movement and muscle coordination.

cruising—When babies walk while holding onto your hands or onto objects in the room.

degenerative—A medical condition that will get worse as the child gets older.

fluctuating muscle tone—Used to describe muscle tone that is a combination of both hypertonic and hypotonic.

handling—Touching, lifting, or manipulating a child with your hands in such a way that the child is more comfortable or is better able to use certain muscles.

hypertonic—Muscle tone that is stiff and rigid.

hypotonic—Low muscle tone in which the child appears "floppy" or "rag-doll" in her movements.

muscle strength—The relative ability of muscles to do tasks that are required for movement and dexterity.

muscular dystrophy—A degenerative condition that results in the child losing muscle strength over time.

partial participation —The concept that if a child is unable due to challenges or limitations to fully participate in an activity then he participates as much as he is able.

spasticity—Stiff or tight muscles with exaggerated or "jerky" movement.

Resources Used in This Chapter

Goswami, U., (ed.). (2004). *Blackwell handbook of childhood cognitive development.* Hoboken, NJ: Blackwell Publishing.

Harper, L. V., & McCluskey, K. S. (2002). Caregiver and peer responses to children with language and motor disabilities in inclusive preschool programs. *Early Childhood Research Quarterly, 17*(2), 148–166.

Martin, S. (2006). *Teaching motor skills to children with cerebral palsy.* Bethesda, MD: Woodbine House.

Segal, M. (1988). *In time with love: Caring for the special needs baby.* New York: New Market Press.

For More Information

Abbott, A., Bartlett, D. J., Kneale Fanning, J. E., & Kramer, J. (2000). Infant motor development and aspects of the home environment. *Pediatric Physical Therapy, 12*(2), 62–67.

Bruni, M. (2006). *Fine motor skills for children with Down syndrome (2nd ed.).* Bethesda, MD: Woodbine House.

Sieglinde, M. (2006). *Teaching motor skills to children with cerebral palsy and similar movement disorders: A guide for parents and professionals.* Bethesda, MD: Woodbine House.

Family Involvement

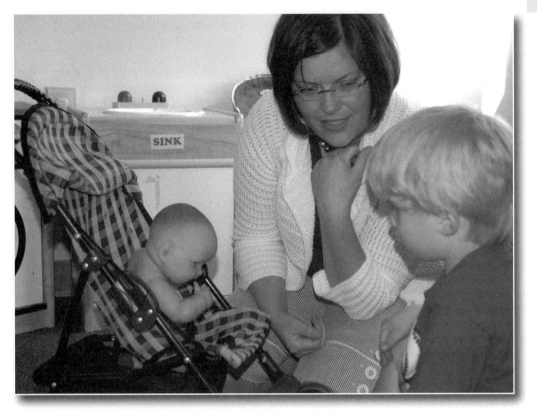

Parents are often a child's first teacher.

Families never expect to have a child with special needs, and each family member will respond differently to the news. However, you can play a vital role in helping families through this adjustment time. Try to provide support, help families learn about the programs and services available to them and recognize that having a child with special needs has an impact on all aspects of family life. Some situations families face include:

- Loss of financial security when one parent is unable to return to work as planned.
- Dealing with well-meaning family members and friends who do not know what to say or say things that are not supportive.
- Feelings of guilt about whether the child's condition is something that could have been prevented.
- Understanding how to navigate the various systems that the child may need to be involved with, such as therapies (speech, physical, occupational), medical appointments, and specialized medical needs.
- Learning how to take care of the child at home while still providing for siblings and other family members.

What Can I Do to Understand a Family's Perspective?

Unless you have a child with disabilities, you can never truly understand the perspective of parents who do. You can sympathize and try to appreciate how parents *might* feel, but you can never really know the day-to-day realities of living with and caring for a young child with disabilities.

For parents of a child with special needs, he is a special, valued, and contributing member of their family. As a teacher, your goal is to help all of the young children in your care become part of the classroom community. You know from experience that all children have strengths and challenges. Some children just happen to have more challenges than others. Parents often agree that the one thing a teacher can do to understand their perspective is to have respect for their opinions and recognize them as valued contributors.

Families are usually aware they have a child who is not like other children. They have likely visited more than one specialist and scoured the Internet searching for information about their child's special needs. They may have accessed a list-serve or visited chat rooms designed for parents of children with special needs; a few may be involved in parent-support groups. Regardless of how much they already know, parents are always looking for more explanations and answers about what they can do to help their child. As a teacher, you can help parents by making sure they know about the resources available to them, including:

- Access to specialists, such as **occupational therapists** or **speech-language pathologists**;
- Information about local support groups for families or siblings;
- Suggestions about where they can obtain information about **adaptive equipment** or **assistive technology**, which are specialized materials for their child);
- Names of community organizations that provide financial support for children with disabilities;
- Government resources that they may be entitled to receive;
- Where to locate **respite care** (a place where the child can go for a day or a few days, so the parents can have a break); and
- Organizations specializing in information about children with special needs.

Disability literature is full of information about the value of enabling and empowering families to become self-advocates. When you enable a family, you give them the tools needed to make informed decisions; when you empower them, you show them how to use those tools. You become an avenue through which parents learn to use the resources and tools available to them to advocate for their child's best interests.

It is important to note that, at various times in a child's life, their family may experience a **cycle of grief and loss** that is not unlike what is experienced when someone dies. The diagnosis of a child with disabilities is compared to this process, because the birth of a child with challenges often represents a death of the parental dreams associated with having a new baby. For example, a parent may realize their child is probably not going to walk, say "mama" or "daddy," learn to ride a bicycle, play sports, be a dancer or cheerleader, get their driver's license, or someday grow up to have children of their own—all significant milestones for parents and children. Determining where a parent is functioning within that grief cycle at the time the child enters your classroom provides a better understanding of the parent's point of view.

What Is the Cycle of Grief and Loss?

The grieving process that a family may experience when they discover their child has a special need has been compared to the grieving process associated with the death of a close relative. This process includes shock, denial, anger, despair, and ultimately, acceptance. It is important to remember that some parents may never experience these stages, others may go through only one or two, and some may go from shock to anger, never moving past anger or staying at that stage for many years. Some families may move forward through the typical steps, in the order they are presented, or they may skip all around as they adjust; there is no clear-cut or expected order.

Parents of children with disabilities never forget about the moment they are told their infant has a disability. Articles written by families of children with disabilities relate the circumstances under which they received the news. Often, mothers receive the information in a medical setting, such as the delivery room—a moment when the mother is mentally, emotionally, and physically drained from giving birth. For less obvious disabilities, such as autism, the diagnosis may be reported in a clinical setting, with little regard for the feelings of the family, where questions about the prognosis for their child or how to best treat him are often answered with medical jargon that parents do not understand.

The goal should be for parents to receive their child's initial diagnosis in a loving and supportive manner by a caring professional who answers their questions with useful information and offers an open-door policy for future questions. In many cases, from the moment a diagnosis is received, parents have access to counselors, early intervention services, and healthcare professionals who help them adjust to and understand the diagnosis. It is not uncommon, however, for a child who has slipped through the cracks to arrive in the classroom without a diagnosis or services. It is beneficial to know your alternatives, as these circumstances will provide opportunities to work with the parents in determining what is best for their child.

No matter how gently a parent is told about their child's disability, it is always a shock. Unlike most childhood illnesses that can be cured with medication or therapy, families must face a situation that is chronic and will not go away. After the initial shock begins to wear off, many parents move into the grief phase known as *denial*. During this phase, the family learns that their *perfect child*, their *gift*, has something wrong. This is especially difficult for families of children with autism, because the diagnosis often takes months or years to determine, while the family copes with the situation on their own with no outside support. While one or both parents may feel that something is *not quite right* with their child, it is not until a diagnosis is confirmed that they begin to face the reality of life with a child with disabilities.

It is not uncommon, at this point, for parents who have been given a diagnosis to seek multiple opinions. In fact, one or both parents may begin *shopping for a cure*, which means they search for anyone or anything that may fix the problem. Families are particularly vulnerable when first learning their child has a disability, and may be victimized by people who prey on their desire to find a cure. Some families borrow heavily against their home to pay for these cures. After exhausting their financial resources, they find there is no *magic pill* to *fix* their child.

During the next phase, parents begin to experience strong emotions, such as anger and despair, and may feel the need to blame someone for their child's disabilities. They frequently experience the feeling that "We are in this alone," with an overwhelming anger at their stressful circumstances. It is during this phase that marriages can be strained, and, as a result, families facing great difficulty may begin to fall apart. One spouse may blame the other for not spending more time at home or not accepting enough responsibility for their child. Self-blame is also common, as a parent (usually the mother) feels she did something wrong during her pregnancy that caused the child to have a disability. The mother of a six-year-old with autism said, "I keep going over and over the things I did when I was pregnant. I painted the baby's room, I pumped my own gas. I had the stomach flu… Did any of these things cause Lee's autism? Did I cause him to be this way?"

Ultimately, most families come to accept the disability as part of who the child is, and learn to appreciate the child for what he *can* do rather than what he *cannot* do. Yet, as the child reaches various milestones in his life (starting school, reaching puberty, and so on), families may revisit one or part of the cycle. Regardless of where parents function within the cycle of grief and loss, or what may be taking place at home, as the child's teacher, you still need the parent's help for the child to have a positive experience in the classroom.

Understanding the Importance of the Family

Teachers must understand that family is important in the lives of young children with special needs. A family is made up of a group of people—either by choice (marriage, adoption, fostering, or guardianship) or by blood—that lives together, supports each other, and grows together. In today's world, a family may be self-defined and include people outside the traditional family unit who serve to support or help the family. The family is the core of a young child's world; all of the people in a child's world are essential and important to his development and success. Families provide a consistent environment of loving acceptance, caring concern, nurturing guidance, and never-ending optimism. However, circumstances may occur where the family environment is not as positive as it could be. According to Helen, the mother of a child with chronic special needs, "I was so busy taking care of my child's physical needs I forgot to take care of him emotionally."

For families of a child with special needs, maintaining this commitment to meet all of his needs is probably the most challenging aspect they face. This is especially true of the child with significant physical or medical needs. Sometimes, if the newborn has spent many months in the hospital before coming home, families feel they have lost critical bonding time with their child. In addition, his special needs may make bonding a challenge. For example, nothing is more rewarding than the first time a family member holds an infant and looks into his eyes. When he looks back, the first step toward bonding and communication has taken place. If the child is blind or has serious medical needs, it may not be possible for those early moments of bonding to take place. As a result, one role you may play is in helping the child's family learn alternative ways to develop a relationship with their infant with special needs.

As the child's teacher, it is essential to recognize, value, and cultivate the child's family and the importance of their involvement. By communicating with a child's family, you can build an alliance that enables the child to have opportunities that extend the learning that happens at school into his home. This is especially important for an infant with special needs, as he will need extra practice to learn new skills.

A child's parents can be your most valuable resource. For example, the child's parents can provide immediate and accurate information regarding their child in terms of what he can do well, what he likes to do, what is challenging for him, and what he dislikes doing. When parents realize their knowledge and opinions are valued, they will welcome the opportunity to share with you what they had to painstakingly learn on their own. Providing opportunities to hear about their experiences can open the door for a smoother transition for their child from home to the classroom.

It is common to hear a value placed on forming a partnership with parents, and important to remember that, in order to enter into any partnership, both parties should have something to contribute to the relationship. By honoring their knowledge and experience, family members offer such a relationship, which can be a win-win opportunity for the child, parent, and teacher. This is especially true regarding the need for consistency between home and the classroom. Thus, focused conversations between teachers and parents become the foundation to achieving effective family involvement.

Barriers to Family Involvement

Recognizing that a child's parents are your best resource regarding the future inclusion of their child in your classroom is only part of the process. The next part is to understand the barriers that may inhibit this necessary involvement. Barriers related to family involvement are numerous, including:

- A family member's previous experiences with care providers,
- Heavy work schedules complicated by constantly missing work because of a child's special needs,
- Lack of gas money for transportation,
- Lack of child care to attend meetings,
- Their child's hectic therapeutic appointments,

- Personal needs and issues unrelated to the child, and
- A perception that the child's teacher is passing judgment on them.

In recognizing the need for family involvement and in understanding the barriers that may prevent it, it is important to remember the degree of family involvement is not an accurate measure of family concern. There is a distinct difference between a family's ability to be involved versus their concern. A family may be very concerned, but limited in the amount of time or money they can offer. If you are willing to be creative regarding how you involve and include parents, you have the opportunity to achieve excellent outcomes. In other words, it is important to meet the parents where they are. Some creative methods for accommodating the needs of a family include:

- Make home visits,
- Send home daily notes about the child's accomplishments or challenges,
- Call the family to discuss the child's progress, and
- Find opportunities to meet outside of traditional "school" hours.

As professionals, you can show respect for and sensitivity to the various challenges and emotions parents experience. Below are 10 simple, but necessary "must-haves" in facilitating successful interactions with families.

10 Communication "Must-Haves" When Working with Families

1. Listen! Listen! Listen! Listen! Listen!

2. Speak politely and positively.

3. Establish partnerships based on mutual trust and respect.

4. Use inviting non-verbal communications and avoid using words like "should" and "ought."

5. Explain information in ways that are understandable.

6. Encourage parents' involvement by asking open-ended questions.

7. Support parents in developing the skills necessary to become strong advocates for themselves and their family.

8. Appreciate cultural diversity.

9. Respect individual differences, desires, needs, and values.

10. Adopt an attitude of equal partnership.

How Do I Let Families Know I Need Their Help?

When you find out that you will have a child with special needs in your class, begin the process of family involvement by including and involving the parents through phone conversations, home visits, and an invitation to your classroom. When you meet the first time, use language that lets families know you respect them. Begin creating a partnership with the sole purpose of planning for what is best for the child. For example:

- Use words like "we" and "us" instead of "me" and "you."
- Talk about their child's challenges, not his weaknesses.
- Ask the families what they think or feel, and then respect what they say.
- Use the child's name when you talk about him.
- Ask about the family's priorities. What would they like to see him accomplish this year?
- Talk with the family about formal supports (professional services) and informal supports (family, friends) they might have.
- Always look for ways to help make all interactions with families a positive experience for both you and the family.

What Can I Do to Make Family Interactions Positive?

Positive interactions with all families are necessary to form a strong partnership and facilitate effective family involvement. To facilitate good interactions, it is important to follow these points throughout the process:

- Plan ahead,
- Develop rapport,
- Foster trust,
- Communicate frequently, and
- Acknowledge and value family input when it is given.

Planning ahead means scheduling conferences and meetings in advance at a time and place convenient to the family. This helps relieve the added stress of missing work, finding a babysitter, or, in some cases, finding someone to transport them to the meeting. Keep conferences short and avoid lengthy discussions about what the child is *not* doing. If possible, talk to the parents beforehand about the purpose of the meeting and who will be attending; use their help to make an agenda for the meeting, allowing a set time for each team member to give input. If parents know the meeting's purpose, they can better prepare. If they have helped plan it, you have truly made them part of the team. Remember to ask the parents if there is anyone else who should be invited and add them to the team. Begin the conference by sharing at least one positive thing about the child. It will not only set the tone for the conference, but it lets parents know you are there for more than just telling them about problems with their child.

The relationship built with a family depends on your rapport. By respecting the family's needs, you indicate that you value their input. Even with different opinions about some aspects of the child's education, you can still share information openly and honestly. Once you establish rapport with a child's family, it is easier to work with them to determine their child's needs and devise a plan to address those needs. Rapport leads to relationships, and relationships help build trust.

Before parents will trust you, they must see that you are worthy of their trust. They want to know you are concerned about their child's well-being and development and will take the steps necessary to create a positive environment for their child. This trust does not come easily or quickly, but once established, you are well on your way to working alongside the parents to make decisions based on the best interest of the child. The purpose of this book is to prepare you for this.

Communicate with parents often and in various ways. Communication provides an on-going association with them and strengthens confidence in their child's progress. A **communication notebook**, which is sent home regularly with the child, is a great way to inform parents about what goes on at school and for parents to communicate what happens at home. Imagine how much easier it will be at school when you know the infant did not sleep well the night before or that he went to bed later than usual.

How Do I Develop This Relationship?

The best way to begin a new relationship with parents or enhance an established one is through listening. Listen to the parents—truly hear what is said—with your ears and your heart. Choose your words carefully and always speak politely. Just as you listen from your heart, also speak from your heart, using words that reflect your understanding of their challenges. This lays the groundwork for establishing a partnership between you and the family. In a partnership, responsibility is shared, all members contribute, and there is no hierarchy of power, because it is understood that parents make the final decision.

Nonverbal communication can be more important than verbal communication; to be authentic, the two components must be reciprocal. At least 70% of any message is delivered nonverbally. Nonverbal communication refers to body language, eyes, posture, and stance, which mirror what you think and feel about what you hear. It is imperative that your body language accurately reflect a positive understanding. For example, lean toward parents during conversations and position your arms open to your sides, never fold your arms across your chest. It is good to make eye contact, smile, and nod, when appropriate. Eye contact in the United States is acceptable. If you are working with families from other cultures, however, the meaning of eye contact may be different and sometimes offensive to the family. Remember, there is no hierarchy in a partnership, so your words should be easily understood by all during meetings or casual conversations. Open-ended questions, in place of yes-or-no questions, are an excellent method for including parents in conversations, as this type of question provides opportunities for more in-depth information sharing.

As the teacher, your interactions lay the groundwork for families to enhance and build confidence in their own advocating skills, which can develop as their child grows and enters the public school system. America is a melting pot of cultural diversity, faced with language and cultural differences; it is important to celebrate and understand the customs and values of children and their families who make up the classroom. As family dynamics change, so must our understanding and methods for working with families. Learn about the beliefs and value systems of families you work with, as this shows respect and commonality. Show that you value individual differences, needs, and desires that parents bring to the table.

Adjusting perceptions may clear the path for better communication between you and parents, leading to more effective parental involvement because parents in your classroom will not feel judged. Finally, listening is mentioned twice because it is essential to family involvement, the partnership, and the level of disclosure between parents and teachers.

The goal is to work with the family to educate their child in a manner consistent with how he learns, and to do so in a way that provides consistency between home and school.

Terms Used in This Chapter

adaptive equipment—Equipment especially designed for a child with special needs that enables him to have more independence.

assistive technology—Any adaptation that is made to an object or an activity that enables the child to complete that activity or use that object more independently.

communication notebook—A series of pictures usually arranged in some predetermined order that is used by a child to communicate his wants, needs, or desires.

cycle of grief and loss—The normal psychological stage of processing grief and loss. It includes shock, denial, anger and guilt, despair and depression, and acceptance.

occupational therapist—A specialist who helps people learn to independently accomplish activities related to work and everyday living, such as bathing, dressing, and other skills.

respite care—Care of a child with special needs, often for several days, to allow the regular caregiver time off.

speech-language pathologist—A specialist who treats speech and language delays.

Resources Used in This Chapter

Wilcox, M. J., Dugan, L. M., Campbell, P. H., & Guimond, A. (2006). Recommended practices and parent perspectives regarding AT use in early intervention. *Journal of Special Education Technology*, 21(4), 7–16.

Willis, C. (2006). *Teaching young children with autism spectrum disorder.* Beltsville, MD: Gryphon House.

For More Information

Bailey, D. B., Jr., Bruder, M. B., Hebbeler, K., Carta, J., Defosset, M., Greenwood, C., et al. (2006). Recommended outcomes for families of young children with disabilities. *Journal of Early Intervention*, 28(4), 227–251.

Dunst, C. J., & Dempsey, I. (2007). Family-professional partnerships and parenting competence, confidence, and enjoyment. *International Journal of Disability, Development and Education*, 54(3), 305–318.

Im, J., Parlakian, R., & Sanchez, S. (2007). Rocking & rolling: Supporting infants, toddlers, and their families. Understanding the influence of culture on caregiving practices… from the inside out. *Young Children*, 62(5), 65–66.

Kondrad, M., Zehr, B., Hanna, C., Rote, V., & Jain, S. (2007). One family's journey: Medical home and the network of supports it offers children and youth with special health care needs, part two—care coordination. *Exceptional Parent*, 37(10), 93–95.

Loewenstein, D. (2007). Increasing our acceptance as parents of children with special needs. *Exceptional Parent*, 37(12), 28–29.

Appendix

Developmental Chart

Age	Skills
Birth–4 months	Displays sensory awareness—see, hear, taste, smell, feel Vision distance at birth—9–14 inches, at 1 month—1–2 feet, at 3 months—6–8 feet Cries to express needs Enjoys social interactions Begins to turn head Makes eye contact Makes cooing sounds Smiles Lifts head to look around Turns head toward a familiar voice Grasps a small object Tracks an object moving from side to side
3–7 months	Reaches Expresses happiness and sadness Supports upper body with arms when on stomach Looks at hands and feet Bats or hits at an object Enjoys looking in a mirror Rolls over Recognizes familiar people Plays "Peek a Boo" Laughs Attempts to pull up Bounces when standing in your lap Holds a bottle
6–10 months	Sits unassisted Looks for an items when dropped Looks for an item when hidden under a pillow Drops things on purpose Changes an object from one hand to the other Rocks on hands and knees Mimics actions

(Continued)

Age	Skills
6–10 months (continued)	Mimics sounds Babbles a string of sounds Pulls up to a standing position Makes purposeful noise Puts small items in mouth Feeds self finger foods Looks at pictures when named Picks things up Pushes and shoves things Crawls
9–13 months	Recognizes familiar words Takes off clothing Fits nesting boxes together Waves goodbye Creeps, scoots, crawls Follows simple directions Looks at a book Remembers where familiar items are kept Drops thing into an open box Scoops items Begins to roll a ball Babbles, mimicking speech Tears paper Copies simple gestures Scribbles Approximates simple words
12–19 months	Moves around the room Plays simple pretend games Puts items in and take them out of a container Uses one-word sentences Plays simple music instruments Hands items to someone Helps dress and undress self Rolls a ball Uses identification words correctly Enjoys looking at a book Retrieves ball that has rolled out of sight Walks upstairs with help Notes differences in temperature, smell, and taste Attempts to sing a song

Developmental Chart (continued)

Age	Skills
12–19 months (continued)	Enjoys messy play Points at familiar objects Hugs and kisses Recognizes self in mirror Stacks two or more blocks Turns two or three pages of a book at a time Tries to kick a ball Shows one or more body parts Pushes, pulls, or carries a toy while walking Places pegs in holes Uses a spoon to scoop
18–36 months	Throws a ball Attempts walking up and down stairs Shows a variety of emotions Chews food Zips and unzips Points to several body parts Walks on wide balance board Rides a small riding toy Enjoys Nursery Rhymes and songs Says two-word sentences Unwraps packages with a little starter help Matches sounds to animals Turns book pages one at a time Enjoys water play Sings word of a song (at least some) Attempts to jump in place Repeats words you say Works a simple puzzle Strings large beads Uses playdough Uses finger paint Holds pictures right side up Uses words that tell what an object does Recognizes self in a picture Runs Listens to a short story Tries to balance on one foot

Adaptive Equipment and Strategies

Adaptive Equipment

Provide adaptive equipment as needed, including:

- Adaptive crayons, paintbrushes, and scissors;
- Finger crayons;
- Mittens for painting;
- Low vision aids;
- Books on tape, in Braille, or that have large print; and
- Therapy balls.

Adaptive Switches

Most battery-operated toys, as well as computer keyboards, are not accessible (user friendly) for children with certain types of special needs. *Adaptive switches* provide an alternate means for children to use toys. Basic switches are used to control the on and off functions of devices, such as tape recorders and battery toys. More sophisticated switches are used to help a child access a computer. The switch can be used either with a device that has been adapted for switch access (such as a special toy) or with an interface (such as a pig-tail adapter) that links the switch to a non-adapted device. Interfaces are inexpensive and are placed next to the battery in the toy and provide a connection to plug the adaptive switch into the toy or recorder.

Types of Adaptive Switches

- Pressure-sensitive switches that require a press, push, or pull action.
- Touch-sensitive switches that respond to a very light touch.
- Air-pressure switches, such as a pneumatic grip switch or a sip-and-puff switch.
- Small muscle sensors that can sense the voluntary movement of a finger, eyebrow, cheek, or other small muscles.
- Infrared beam switches that respond to movement within their "field of vision."
- Sound-sensitive switches.

Adaptive Handles

Adaptive handles are used to help a child pick up an object. There are many ways to adapt handles, including:

1. Attach foam hair rollers, like those used to curl hair, to the handle of objects creating handles that are easier to grasp.
2. Securing a few crayons together with rubber bands creates a "crayon" that is easier for some children to use.
3. Wrap a few rubber bands around an object, including a single crayon or marker, making the object easier to grasp and handle.
4. Tape metal nuts to a pencil to give it more weight.

Page Turners

Page turners are used to help a child more easily turn a page in a book. Try one of the following ideas:

1. Attach a wooden clothespin to each page. This gives the child a handle to hold when turning the pages.
2. Place a dot of hot glue on the upper left-hand corner of each page. Wait for each dot to cool, before going to the next page.
3. Attach a metal paperclip to the top left-hand corner of each page. This provides something for the child to grasp.

Desk or Tabletop Easel

This can be used with a child with visual or motor issues. The tabletop easel is used to help the child see a book or a written activity.

1. Get a sturdy cardboard box.
2. Cut the top of the box. Then, cut the box in half, along the diagonal shown in the illustration.
3. Place each half of the box on its open end, creating two tabletop easels.
4. Cut two slits along the peak, where you can insert clothespins to secure paper to the easel.
5. If the easel slides around too much, place a book or other heavy object in the bottom section or place it on a piece of non-slip material, such as scatter-rug backing.

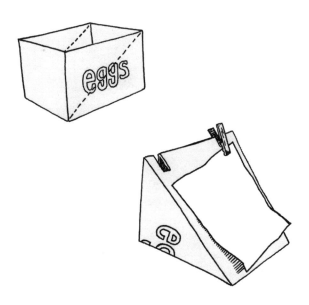

Teaching Infants, Toddlers, and Twos with Special Needs

Index